YOUR GOD M̲   ̲ALL

YOUR GOD MAY BE TOO SMALL
Misleading Descriptions of God that Disaffect Us

Nicholas Ayo, csc

YOUR GOD MAY BE TOO SMALL
Misleading Descriptions of God That Disaffect Us

10 9 8 7 6 5 4 3 2

ISBN: 978-0-9912451-1-6

Published by
CORBY BOOKS
A Division of Corby Publishing, LP
P.O. Box 93 ~ Notre Dame, IN 46556
(574) 784-3482

Distributed by
ACTA Publications
4848 N. Clark Street, Chicago, IL 60640.
800-397-2282
www.actapublications.com

Manufactured in the United States of America

DEDICATED TO THE MEMORY OF

JOHN SCRIVENER DUNNE, C.S.C.
1929-2013
Author, Teacher, Mentor, Colleague, Friend,
Priest, Brother in Holy Cross

ACKNOWLEDGEMENTS

So many persons over the years could be mentioned as the support that enables an author to write a book. The Corby Breakfast Club and the "usual suspects" in the Corby Hall morning routine brightened every day before the writing began. I want to thank the following people by name, who were with me in the beginnings of this book: Lyn Pusztai, Anne Luther, Alida Macor, John Macor, Mary Catherine Rowland, John Chaplin, and as so often, my editor, James Langford.

All Biblical quotations are taken from the New Revised Standard Version.

TABLE OF CONTENTS

1. God Is Never Angry or Disappointed –
   God Is Always Happy And Joyful.............................. 1
2. God Is Never Imposing or Controlling –
   God Is Always Enabling.. 6
3. God Is Not Lonely, Isolated or Deprived –
   God Is Personal.. 11
4. God Is Not Supercilious or Over-bearing –
   God Is Gracious.. 16
5. God Is Never Absent – God Is Always Present............... 20
6. God Is Never Aloof or Uninvolved –
   God Is Engaged Among Us.................................... 24
7. God Is Never Disabled – God Is Infinitely Resourceful..... 32
8. God Is Never Worried or Frustrated –
   God Is Father Almighty and Sovereign Providence...... 37
9. God Is Never Changing r Wavering –
   God Is Ever Faithful.. 43
10. God Is Never Judgmental or Punitive –
    God Is Ever Merciful.. 49

11. God Is Not Heartless –
    God Is Love and Nothing Less.................................... 62
12. In God There Is No Darkness –
    God Is Light and Truth... 67
13. God Is Not The God of The Dead –
    God Is God of the Living... 72
14. No One Has Seen God –
    God Is Revealed in Jesus of Nazareth.......................... 78
15. The Eucharist Is Not Embarrassing –
    The Eucharist Is Only Misunderstood.......................... 82
16. God Is Not Finished with Us Yet –
    God Has Come and Is Still to Come............................ 89
17. God Is Never Noisy or Wordy –
    God Is Silent and of Few Words................................. 94
18. God Is Not Complicated – God Is Simply One................ 99
19. God Is Not Comparable to Anything –
    God Is Unique Mystery...105
20. God Is Not Comprehendible – God Is Ineffable...............111
21. God Is Not the Problem –
    God Is the Solution...115
Epilogue..123

Introduction

Why was this book written? Two reasons prevail in my mind. I hope to reach two readers. The first reader might believe in God and also might believe in Jesus as the revelation of God, but that person does not feel close to God. A large part of the reason is that God, even seen in Jesus, seems unapproachable. I want to persuade that reader that God is lovely and easy to be with. The second reader may well be a searcher seeking God and hoping there is a God, or maybe hoping not, but that person is likely estranged from God or does not at all believe in God, because their image of God does not deserve belief from anyone. I want to persuade the reader to reconsider God.

With a nudge from the reading of the Bible, we think

that we human beings are made in the image of God, and quite fatally for our enlightenment and our happiness we return the favor. We make God in our own image. And such a flawed image of God raises skeptics and alienates us from God. Misleading or mistaken descriptions of God disaffect us.

From the start I know that no arguments can convince someone that God can be known and is worth knowing. Faith in God and love for God are the result of God's grace; yet, God's grace is given to everyone everywhere all the time, although such grace is not always recognized.

I would further claim that we do not know where in our heart of hearts, where in our deepest heart, we have our relationship with God. We do not know the depths of ourselves. Only God knows us in that deep heart. The skeptics and the alienated need not despair, or assume they have it all figured out as a zero, for they may be very surprised at what God has accomplished within them. Similarly, the believer should not be presumptuous. Because one knows the language, practices a religion, says one's prayers explicitly does not tell the whole story of what may or may not be going on in the depths of one's heart.

The word "God" means different things to different people. With the help of theological reasoning and a judicious construal of various Biblical passages I try to describe God with as much thoughtfulness as I can achieve. I will use passages from the Bible as illustrations of what I conclude, rather than as proof. I am aware that you can prove most anything in the Bible if you cherry-pick your passages. Proof-texting never persuades. For example, the prophet Isaiah tells us to hammer our swords into plowshares (2:4) and the prophet Joel tells us a time has come to hammer our plowshares into swords (3:10). You will not prove anything about war and peace by simply choosing Biblical texts in your favor. I must hope that my readers will see the cogency of what I describe God not to be and what I describe God to be, even though God far exceeds human description.

I am not sure that I have ever met an atheist. I have talked with some persons who claimed to be atheists, but when I asked them to tell me what they meant by God, I could not believe in such a God either. I know there are many agnostics, who are not sure there is a God or much of anything about God. I greatly admire them and sometimes want to say, "count me in as well." And yet, I do believe in God, as a grace and a gift given to me, and I do not think the less of those still in search of God. To those who are sure there is no God, such as they conceive God to be, I want to say "how can you be so sure"? Almost surely your God is too small. To try to say something about God that gives God a better chance to win the hearts and minds of men and women is why I thought to write about what God is not like and what God is like, assuming, of course, that I can tell the difference, however imperfectly, between helpful and unhelpful talk about God.

What I hope to describe is a God worthy of belief and more than worthy. So much is at stake. If there is a loving God, who loves each and every one of us, really and truly, everything changes. The whole world has life and hope of eternal happiness, if we all are truly in the hands of an infinite God. Finite god(s) would be no god(s) at all. If we conclude, "I cannot believe in God," I hope at least it is with a sad sigh rather than with a "thank God" (scratch that) a "thank goodness." Everything is at stake if there is God and what God is like. One can wait and see, and in fact we all must wait and see. Some anxiety and uncertainty will plague us all in our journey through life with at best a mysterious God. I want to say "thank God," for a God I could fully comprehend might not be much of a God.

Imagine this from your travel agent. Suppose you were offered a trip--length depending and somewhat undetermined -- an excursion, destination planet earth. Imagine a walk, long or short, in space and time, and God was to be your tour guide, not too visible to distract you, and by and by your companion whom you would come to know and even love. God will wait for us; we will catch up with God, and that should not be threatening to us. God is gracious, as we will describe later on, but I think it would be so sad that I missed my walk with God because the world distracted me or because I wanted to be on my own, just a bit bothered by it all.

What's not to like about God? Why are many persons turned away from God? What understanding or misunderstanding of God prevails in the common currency of talk about God? If I say I do not believe in God, I presume to know something about what God is like. What God is like I say I dislike, which makes it easier to reject such an unattractive God or to propose a denial there is any such God, and if there were, I want no part in that God, who is probably a fiction anyway.

Suppose we try to paint the rejected God. Three common and recurrent complaints come to mind. (1) God is uninteresting to us in himself. He lives a whole different life. We don't understand God; God does not understand us. We are just not in the same world. God is too big, too distant, too inhuman, invulnerable, never needy, all too perfect—just too much and a bit boring. (2) God is useless, unnecessary, not helpful, unwilling or impotent to intervene, mercurial, silent, seemingly indifferent. We are left to ourselves whether there is a God or not. Paradoxically, God is thought to be controlling all things and all people. From "in the beginning" God is dominating and imposing himself on human freedom. His demands are everlasting, but any assistance remains unpredictable and all too absent to our eyes. (3) God is threatening, punitive, and even vindictive "in the ending" of this unasked-for world from "in the beginning." We fear a God that is judgmental, whose surveillance is omnipresent, who is punishing and even violent. The master-servant model does not go down with us. I want to be me. No God, thank you. In short, we don't like God, and such a God does not deserve our belief. On the part of believers in God the answer to such objections is that they do not believe in such an unlikeable God either.

So, what is God like? I suggest we begin each chapter with what God is not like, for we see better when the darkness of misunderstanding is cleared away. We human beings are quick to sing a song off-note, and then to say we don't like that song or the song is no good. So, what is God really like, and what is God not like, so that our misunderstandings do not cement our unbelief and disaffection. Properly spoken about, God just may be irresistible or at least suggestive that I should not be so sure. I may even secretly hope such a likeable God might just be believeable after all.

CHAPTER ONE

God Is Never Angry or Disappointed – God Is Always Happy and Joyful

That God is always joyful, happy, and infinitely fulfilled seems to me the place to begin to understand in a helpful way what God is like. God is always benevolent, generous, loving, for God is Love. God is Bliss. God is never upset, disappointed in us, angry, or morose. Only we are so, and God also when we make God in our own image. That we remind ourselves that God must be and is infinitely good, true, and beautiful, without any hostility, diminution, or vulnerability is important for two reasons. (1) Such an understanding cuts us down to human size. Who do we think we are that we could make God unhappy or angry, much less make God happy and at peace supremely? In doing evil or good we have no such power. (2) If we could impact God's life and its joy, then we would have reason to believe God's love for us, and the joy God takes in us, depends in some measure on our behavior. If I can anger God, maybe I should worry whether or not God's love for me remains, as I thought, unconditional and gratuitous, infinitely generous and un-failing, whether I do good or do bad, am saint or villain. God's love is boundless and all-inclusive. God loves us not because we are good, but because God is good. And forever may it be so. Were God's love to depend on me and my behavior, we do have reason to worry. If there is a God who loves as we human beings all too often love, there is reason to worry. God is not, however, made in our image. God does not reward good and punish evil like we do, who react to what others do. God is goodness and love that are way out in front of the first glimmerings of our motivations and behaviors for better or for worse. A God who is unchanging and unchangeable offers a love that is unchanging and unchangeable, and that is a believable God worth believing in.

Consequently, if God is not made happy by my good behavior nor unhappy by my bad behavior, should

I conclude that God is indifferent to my behavior? Not at all, but I still want to say that God does delight in me whatever my behavior. Sin hurts the sinner most of all as the first and most serious victim, and if God loves us he would have us unhurt. My bad behavior hurts me and those around me. God knows that and is not indifferent or inactive in the remediation of my misery. God will have the last word -- not me. The joyfulness of God will prevail, because creation itself and all its providential evolution remain always in the hand of God, who has no "future" that God is waiting for. We await "the ending" and our ending, and often needing and wanting pity. God lives "in the ending," that like "in the beginning" is found to be "very good." God has no past and no future. God is all Now –- all present, all seen, all known, all loved. God is not in time past or time future. We are in time —-past, present, and future -- that God created "in the beginning" and which will cease "in the ending." Both the beginning and the ending of our lives are all an eternal now to God.

What we know is that the whole blooming buzzing world is a divine comedy and not a divine tragedy, which is not to say that the story is all laughs, but rather to insist that the story has a happy ending. How happy and for how many, you may ask? Will God wipe away all our tears and make it all come out right in the end for everyone? We should surely hope so, and we may hope so. There is mighty reason to believe God's love trumps all else.

An objection can be made that all emotions attributed to God are a distortion based on our own bodily existence. We have emotions because we have a body that reacts to hormones, chemicals, electrical nerve discharges, and a world of material input in sequential fashion. God is spirit and technically speaking God cannot be as we can be -- angry, sad, happy, hurt, peaceful, tired, hungry, randy, bored or surprised. Consequently, God is never frustrated, disappointed, or lacking what human beings enjoy. God does not miss the taste of sugar or the sound of music. All of reality God possesses in an eminent way. God does not need to change, for if one is already everything that could be, there is no more to be added to infinity. God is not developing, nor lacking, nor vulnerable. God is all in all at once and forever. The Bible personifies God in its many narratives, and he appears to have emotions like us, but bigger and better. However, one should not take any Biblical depiction of God as without need of some theological commentary.

Of Wisdom personified we read:

> The Lord created me at the beginning of his work, the first of his acts of long ago. Ages ago I was set up, at the first, before the beginning of the earth. When there were no depths I was brought forth, when there were no springs abounding with water. Before the mountains had been shaped, before the hills, I was brought forth – when he had not yet made earth and fields, or the world's first bits of soil. When he established the heavens, I was there, when he drew a circle on the face of the deep, when he made firm the skies above, when he established the fountains of the deep, when he assigned the sea its limit, so that the waters might not transgress his command, when marked out the foundations of the earth, then I was beside him, like a master worker; and I was daily his delight, rejoicing before him always, rejoicing in his inhabited world and delighting in the human race (Prov 8: 22-31).

Chapter Two

God Is Never Imposing or Controlling – God Is Always Enabling

Because God is supremely free and self-assured within himself, God has no wish or need to dominate others, whom he has created. Creation itself adds nothing to God's glory, which is and always will be infinite. Creation is God's gratuitous gift, for our sake and not for his. Creation is God's overflowing love, a love and joy God wants to share and not in any way impose. God lacks nothing. He does not need us to be his servants or slaves and to do his will on earth, as if he were impotent to provide for his creation of a world. Though God does not need us, God offers us to be co-creators, and he invites us to collaborate with him in the work of creation and salvation so that we might have a part and, in our own way, offer life and salvation to others. God does not need our help, but invites it for our own sake. God sustains an agenda of his own, but God does ask our free collaboration. Hence pro-creation.

We often think that "God's will" must be done. We must discover and carry out God's will for us. God has a path I must walk in obedience to God's will. "Thy will be done on earth as it is in heaven," as we pray in the Lord's Prayer. That conclusion gives a wrong impression. God has no contrived plan for me or anyone else. Like a loving parent, God wants me to find my own special gifts and lead my own chosen life. What God does want, and what any good parent wants, is just this. God wants me to be me, and God wants me to do what I want to do, but provided that what I choose comes from the real me, the God-given me with gifts unique, and not from the propaganda of the surrounding very ungodly culture I live in. So often what we think we want to do to be true to ourselves is but an echo or mimetic desire that sees what others are doing and is brain-washed into concluding I must want to do the same things or should want to do them. If the culture around me suggests the good life is one with wealth and privilege, I may think that must be the life I want. Again, our God may be too small and our own estimation of God's gift to me may also be too small. Coming to know who I am and what at the deepest level of my being I want to do with my life is what God's will is for me – nothing more and nothing less. In that sense God is saying to us all that he will go with us wherever we go, whatever path we take, even provisional paths and wrong paths that can lead with God's gentle companionship to right paths. "Wherever you go, I will go" says Naomi to Ruth in that wonderful Biblical story of a loyal and enduring commitment to companionship. "The Lord is my shepherd," but he does not have a leash on me. He goes where I go, and he leads me in right paths to green pastures. I am allowed to surprise God in what I choose to do with my life, and he delights that I discover my way, even if he has been at work in me with his grace all along, illuminating my mind with his truth and enkindling my heart with his love.

Christians claim that God walked among us as one of us, made flesh at Bethlehem and crucified in Jerusalem. We somehow thought his love for us in his gospel ways was lost to us. God, however, has not left us in the world without his on-going real presence. His companionship is real, but any imposition of his will upon us is not real. The controlling God remains our misunderstanding of God, a

God that we think has to be in control to be God. God acts through our own freedom, our true freedom, not to be confused with the license and indulgence sold us by a materialistic culture all too often. "And remember, I am with you always, to the end of the age" (Mt 28: 20). God would echo Shakespeare's line "To your own self be true, and thou then canst be false to no man." Jesus thought the domination of rules and the will of man was not in our best interest. "The Sabbath was made for man, not man for the Sabbath." Our flourishing is the only thing that the will of God is interested in, but our true and genuine flourishing. St. Irenaeus said it well in his oft-quoted phrase: "The glory of God is man fully alive."

> The day was drawing to a close, and the twelve came to him and said, "Send the crowd away, so that they may go into the surrounding villages and countryside, to lodge and get provisions; for we are here in a deserted place." But he said to them, "*You give them something to eat.*" [italics mine] They said, "We have no more than five loaves and two fish – unless we are to go and buy food for all these people." For there were about five thousand men. And he said to his disciples, "Make them sit down in groups of about fifty each." They did so and made them all sit down. And taking the five

9

loaves and the two fish, he looked up to heaven, and blessed and broke them, and gave them to the disciples to set before the crowd. And all ate and were filled. What was left over was gathered up, twelve baskets of broken pieces. (Lk 9: 12-17)

CHAPTER THREE

God Is not Lonely, Isolated or Deprived – God Is Personal

I want to say it is important not to think of God as deprived in any way. God is not lonely or isolated, and if he were we might have reason to worry about a God that should be not at all like us. Loneliness and isolation for human beings verge on the essence of a kind of hell. Solitary confinement may be the harshest of punishments devised for mankind.

In my foolish assumption that I could stand in God's shoes in any way, I would worry God might be lonely were God all by himself alone in God's kingdom, or whatever foolish word I should be putting here for God's whereabouts. We would not know of the infinitely rich inter-personal life of God, were it not for what we are told of God by the Word of God made flesh in Jesus Christ. Christians claim to know something more than what theists who believe in the awesome but unknown God want to claim. However imperfectly we can comprehend God's ultimate identity; we think it to be unique personal relationships.

To greatly simplify at the risk of misleading myself and my reader, I want to say we could well think of God as a family – Father, Son, and Holy Spirit. God is a community, a community of divine Persons in complete mutual love one for the other. That love is fully given and fully received, and that continues to be exchanged in what is incomparable joy in love and love in joy. There exists at the heart of "who God is" a melody of "Persons," endowed with the divine essence that is infinite existence itself. God is infinitely endowed with personal love and companionship and all else. Of nothing is God deprived, and anything our created world could boast, God is and has in his being, regardless of his creation of all of us. We have then but begun to describe God's personal life.

God wants nothing from us in the miracle and great mystery of our creation, i.e., if God is everything, how can anything be something? God wants only to share God's all with us. Similarly, if we are somehow invited into the mystery of God's personal relationships, that is over and above creation. That is creation squared, that intimacy is over the top, that is the intimacy and inner mystery of God's love given us to share with God in the happiness of eternal life in the world to come. If you say it is too good to be true, I would have sympathy. It surely is a stretch. But if you reject God because his supposedly lonely life, sung to by angels with harps sitting on the clouds of heaven, sounds to you boring and unappealing, I would also have sympathy with you. I would point out, however, that your God might just be too small.

If human beings are made in the image of God, as Christians believe, then we were made in the image of the Trinitarian God. There is only one God, yet the Father is not the Son, nor the Holy Spirit as the Love between them commingled with them. There remains only one God.

Even in our own way we human persons are many and yet one. I am not you, and you are not me; yet I am you and you are me. I have borders but no boundaries. Nations have borders but no boundaries. Weather and contagion affect the whole globe as one planet earth. We are somehow members of each other, members of the body of Christ, and just as the liver is not the heart, yet they are both me and I am one body, so I am you and you are me. That is why we could all sin in Adam and all be saved in Jesus, who prays to his Father: "I in them and Thou in me" (Jn 17: 23).

> But now I am coming to you, and I speak these things in the world so that they may have my joy made complete in themselves. I have given them your word, and the world has hated them because they do not belong to the world, just as I do not belong to the world. I am not asking you to take them out of the world, but I ask you to protect them from the evil one. They do not belong to the world. Sanctify them in the truth; your word is truth. As you have sent me into the world, so I have sent them into the world. And for their sakes I sanctify myself , so that they also may be sanctified in truth. I ask not only on behalf of these, but also on behalf of those who will believe in me through their word, that they may all be one. As you, Father, are in me and I am in you, may they also be in us, so that the world may believe that you have sent me. The glory that you have given me I have given them so that they may be one, as we are one, I in them and you in me, that they may become completely one, so that the world may know that you have sent me and have loved them even as you have loved me. Father,

I desire that those also, whom you have given me may be with me where I am to see my glory which you have given me because you loved me before the foundation of the world (Jn 17: 13-25).

Chapter Four

God Is Not Supercilious or Over-bearing -- God is Gracious

God is not uncomfortable to be around. Julian of Norwich insisted in her writing that God was "gracious." God would make visitors comfortable. God was a gentleman who would meet others where they were in their lives. He could talk to anyone, break bread with anyone, hear anyone's silent speech, and be at home with anyone. God was consummate compassion for the human condition and for us human beings. He loved us and cared to know our plight, and we believe God joined us most intimately and walked with us from birth to death through all its vicissitudes and hazards of time and place. God has good reason, especially the God whom Christians proclaim, to be empathetic and sympathetic to any and all of the "thousand slings and arrows that mortal flesh is heir to."

Creation itself is lavish, even prodigal, more than ample. God gained nothing from creation but would give us everything that God's infinite riches could bestow. His love is gratuitous and unconditional -- a pure love for the sake of the beloved. His gift of life and love has no strings attached. He would never embarrass the recipients of his largesse, because his attitude is naught but gracious -- kind and considerate in every way. God is a joy to be around, a delight to be with, a treasure to know and love.

This tenderness of God is made clearly manifest in the life of Jesus, whom Christians believe reveals in human ways the face of God. For Christians Jesus is the revelation of the Father Almighty translated into human behavior that is most sensitive to our predicaments. He noticed the widow whose only son was being buried, and he raised him to life for her. He noticed the widow's mite, the small coin that was all she had, which she was willing to give to the Temple collection. Jesus was like her and with her in generosity and self-donation. When he encounters our death for the first time in the Gospel of John he weeps at the tomb of his friend, Lazarus. Jesus did not "out" Judas as a villain, whose betrayal may well have been part of a plan to start an insurrection to free Israel with the arrest of Jesus as the match to start the fire. Though the plot went wrong, Jesus did not tie the hands of Judas nor run from him. "Let him who is without sin cast the first stone" may sound like a strategy to save the woman taken in adultery from a brutal stoning to death by an angry mob of righteous men, but Jesus wanted not so much to embarrass the men publicly as to save the men themselves from committing cruel violence upon a helpless woman that they would subsequently regret. Jesus was nothing but gracious. Only hypocrisy raised anger.

> Now when Jesus returned, the crowd welcomed him, for they were all waiting for him. Just then there came a man named Jairus, a leader of the synagogue. He fell at Jesus' feet and begged him to come to his house, for he had an only daughter, about twelve years old, who was dying. As he went, the crowds pressed in on him. Now there was a woman who had been suffering from hemorrhages for twelve years; and though she had spent all she had on physicians, no one could cure her. She came up behind him and touched the fringe of his clothes, and immediately her hemorrhage stopped. Then Jesus

asked, "Who touched me?" When all denied it, Peter said, "Master, the crowds surround you and press in on you." But Jesus said, "Someone touched me; for I noticed that power had gone out from me." When the woman saw that she could not remain hidden she came trembling; and falling down before him, she declared in the presence of all the people why she had touched him, and how she had been immediately healed. He said to her, "Daughter, your faith has made you well; go in peace."

While he was still speaking someone came from the leader's house to say, "Your daughter is dead; do not trouble the teacher any longer." When Jesus heard this, he replied, "Do not fear. Only believe, and she will be saved." When he came to the house, he did not allow anyone to enter with him, except Peter, John, and James, and the child's father and mother. They were all weeping and wailing for her; but he said, "Do not weep; for she is not dead but sleeping." And they laughed at him, knowing that she was dead. But he took her by the hand and called out, "Child, get up!" Her spirit returned, and she got up at once. Then he directed them to give her something to eat" (Lk 8: 40-55).

CHAPTER FIVE

God Is Never Absent — God Is Always Present

God is omnipresent as well as ubiquitous. God is really present in both time and space, really here and now. God is not ever gone from the world, never "absent without leave" from creation. God is here and there, everywhere. And God is everywhere all of the time, not just in the past or only coming in the future. "Waiting for Godot" is not waiting for God unless one means waiting for recognition that the real presence of God here and now, in space and time, is really God. God is always and everywhere with us -- Emmanuel (God-with-us), as the

Hebrew Scriptures long ago surmised. If God were absent but for a moment or for a tiny space we would fall out of existence, for it is God's presence that is our being, though in the mystery of creation we do not hold that we are God made manifest or some part of God in the world. God is more me than I am, and yet I am me and I am not God. St. Paul quotes an ancient poet of some wisdom who speaks of God: "In him we move and live and have our being." In short, God is always present in time, because God has no beginning and no ending, and time itself is God's creation that could not sustain itself in existence without the presence of God every moment. God is always present in space, because God has no limitations that stem from a material existence and space itself is God's creation that could not sustain itself in existence without the presence of God anywhere and everywhere.

Christians talk of the "real presence" of Jesus Christ in the bread of the Eucharist. Tabernacles in Christian churches are accompanied with an ever-burning sanctuary candle to remind the faithful who visit the church that God is present, really present. "Real presence" is mostly a spatial metaphor. Christians may be tempted to think Jesus is not so present a mile away from the tabernacle, or not so present in the breaking of bread in their homes compared to the mystery on their altars. Such understanding is too narrow and discounts the "real presence" of Jesus who is with the Father, one God and not two, and always and everywhere present in space and time. What is often overlooked is this. "Real presence" is not just a spatial metaphor, but it is also a temporal metaphor. God has entered our world and has not gone away, just because the brief years that Jesus walked this earth have faded away in memory. Jesus came to stay. God in Jesus is as much involved in our lives as ever. We may think we are disadvantaged because we cannot see the real presence of God in Jesus walking around, but those who lived with Jesus did not recognize the real presence of God any more than we tend to do in our time and place. It was only with the eyes of faith that they recognized his presence in their midst, and that recognition came days, weeks, and years after he was no longer seemingly with them. God is with us, and those who cultivate their interior life have seen him, not to photograph him, but to know and love the "real presence" of the God forever engaged with this our world.

> The Lord is my shepherd, I shall not want.
> He makes me lie down in green pastures.
> He leads me beside still waters.

He restores my soul.

He leads me in right paths for his names sake.

Even though I walk through the darkest valley, I fear no evil, for you are with me.

Your rod and your staff – they comfort me.

You prepare a table before me in the presence of my enemies.

You anoint my head with oil; my cup overflows.

Surely goodness and mercy shall follow me all the days of my life,

And I shall dwell in the house of the Lord my whole life long.

Ps 23

For we are the temple of the living God; as God said, "I will live in them and walk among them, and I will be their God, and they shall be my people."

2 Cor 6:16

CHAPTER SIX

God Is Never Aloof or Uninvolved – God Is Engaged Among Us

If we talk about what is possible, the world constructed by many scientists will say that this wild universe and beautiful planet earth could be explained without God, for the evolutionary potential of the stuff of the cosmos seems to be both enormous and surprisingly complex and full of wonder. Into this great amazement we surely should put ourselves, even were human beings not alone in the vast unknown reaches of stellar space in a universe still expanding. If we talk about what is probable, however, such as winning the lottery, the world that supports our body and the earth that is our home seem to be a very unlikely amalgamation of so many things that had to go right and so many ways for each of them to go wrong. For example, take the temperature on the surface of the earth – a bit colder and the oceans freeze and a bit warmer and they boil away. Our fireplace is ninety-three million miles away and not at all in our control. The earth spins conveniently at one thousand miles an hour to distribute the sun's rays. Could be all chance. God knows there are billions of galaxies each with billions of stars and no doubt many planets, and if a monkey threw up the letters of the alphabet innumerable times, sooner or later (and probably later) they would all come down as the complete plays of Shakespeare. Possible, all possible, but without something or someone more probable, the odds that blind chance explains all of us remain astronomical, and the adjective is aptly chosen.

Creation itself remains God's perpetual gift renewed every moment less we fall back into nothingness. God does hold us all in the palm of his hand. We have not much reason to believe in or hope for a God who created a world that is fragile, needy, and vulnerable and then walked way aloof like a deadbeat dad. God holds creation up, if there is a God worthy of the best meaning of that word.

"I believe in God, the father almighty" tries to say God is love (father) that is power (almighty) and power that is love. One without the other will prove a disaster, as we know from human history.

Given God's infinite riches God could afford to be lavish in creation, and what we have given is surely lavish. We are richly blessed or we are unbelievably lucky. Winning the lottery does not come even close. Given the awesome beauty of our planet in this vast universe, given the thousands of flowers of such astonishing variety and beauty, given the mountains, clouds, rivers, and oceans in their wonder, and our body so supple and our mind so wondering of the mysteries within and without, one wants to say "thank you" for what feels like a magnanimous over-the-top gift that is human life here and now. As Annie Dillard so aptly said: "We would have been satisfied with so much less."

If there is a God, we are surely his creation, for a God worthy of the name has no rival. Demi-gods will not explain us. Only the one God who is God because self-explained, not derived, not lacking any power or being, supreme, makes any real sense as true god. Rival gods could only be demi-gods, for what one has the other would not have.

Let us argue that God is engaged with God's creation always and everywhere. He is never uninvolved or aloof. Moreover, if God became enfleshed in Jesus, as Christians believe, then God's involvement is yet more profound and permanent. As the saying about commitment goes: "you have to have skin in the game." Here is the problem that God's generosity and involvement with us presents to God. If God chooses to love us who are his creation made capable of knowing and loving him in return in some measure, God must not scare us with a courtship that leaves us no breath of our own.

Soren Kierkegaard tells a story of God that is the epitome of a claim for the sensitivity of God. Accordingly, a King falls in love with a peasant maiden, whom he now wishes to marry. As King he can do what he wants, and even if his court resents his marrying beneath his dignity, the king is king and can marry the poor maiden of his choice. He hesitates because of a gracious concern for her. She will become queen; she will go from rags to riches. However, she will be forever indebted to him to whom she will owe everything. The king wants her love freely given and for himself alone and not for his riches. So, the king is distressed until he decides upon this plan. He will disguise himself as a humble peasant and court the maiden he loves. Alas, the plan is flawed. She will have to know sooner or later that he is the king. One more plan comes to mind. He could abdicate the throne, become a humble peasant, and court the maiden he loves as her equal. But, the king has a concern. If he is but a humble peasant gone a-courting, she may turn him down. Or, she may have preferred to be a rich queen even though indebted. And so the king's love is an unhappy love, a thoughtful love that depends on a human response that he will not force and which he would not want for a moment to require unless love from the heart were freely given.

In reality, God chose to approach us as one of us, as a child born of a woman, born in obscurity and poverty in a land under stress from its circumstances as well as from world politics that controlled it. Jesus spent some thirty years in a small village in Galilee called Nazareth, and we know next to nothing about how he spent his time. We do know that ordinary human life with its joys and sorrows was not below his dignity, and that the earth and all of human behavior has been colored with its potential to be touched by God made flesh. In the Christian understanding of the incarnation of the Son of God the implication is that all of this world in space and time is now sacramental and capable of being in the presence of God who has taken the world to himself in an irrevocable way. We believe Jesus had to learn how to talk and walk, that he had to manage his toe nails as anyone else, and that he had no special information from on high about future events or what he was to do beyond what help could be found in prayer and meditation. He spent his time in the marketplace with ordinary folks, sinners and saints like, and not on the mountain top away from the turmoil. He had a special care for widows and orphans, an atypical respect and love for the women he encountered in a patriarchal world, and a deep appreciation for the "lilies of the field that toil not, neither do they spin, and yet I say to you that even Solomon in all his glory was not arrayed like one of these" (Mt 6: 28-29).

Jesus claimed he was "the bread of life," and his solidarity with us is as basic to our life as bread that keeps us alive. In him our mortality and God's immortality were joined. God in Jesus loved human beings in their bodily existence. He ate with everyone, rich and poor, friend and foe, sinner and saint. He multiplied the loaves and the fishes, changed water into large jars of wine at the wedding feast, cooked a meal of bread and fish for his disciples' breakfast after a night of futile fishing on the Lake of

Galilee. That he would in a mysterious way stay with us as bread, as sacrament most holy, as "This is my body, given for you," should come as no surprise. He was our companion (cum-panis , i.e., with bread) then and now, the one we break bread with and who accompanies us on our each day's journey. "Give us this day our daily bread" offers so many meanings.

Jesus gave no answer in words to the perennial problem and complaint about human suffering, but he did heal the sick and console the afflicted, and he did promise his presence: "Lo, I am with you always, even unto the end of the world" (the last words of Matthew's Gospel).

> We know that all things work together for good for those who love God, who are called according to his purpose. For those whom he foreknew he also predestined to be conformed to the image of his Son, in order that he might be the firstborn within a large family. And those whom he has predestined he also called; and those whom he called he also justified; and those whom he justified he also glorified. What then are we to say about these things? If God is for us, who is against us? He who did not withhold his own Son, but gave him up for all of us, will he not with him also give us everything else? Who will bring any charge against God's elect? It

is God who justifies. Who is to condemn? It is Christ Jesus, who died, yes, who was raised, who is at the right hand of God, who indeed intercedes for us. Who will separate us from the love of Christ? Will hardship, or distress, or persecution, or famine, or nakedness, or peril, or sword? As it is written, "For your sake we are being killed all day long; we are accounted as sheep to be slaughtered." No, in all these things we are more than conquerors through him who loved us. For I am convinced that neither death, nor life, nor angels, nor rulers, nor things present, nor things to come, nor powers, nor height, nor depth, nor anything else in all creation, will be able to separate us from the love of God in Christ Jesus our Lord (Rm 8: 28-39).

CHAPTER SEVEN

God Is Never Disabled
– God Is Infinitely Resourceful

God is infinite. God is not limited in any way. God is infinitely resourceful. Everything belongs to God and is at his disposal without compromising the integrity of anything or anyone. In short, what God wants, God gets. God is never disabled. Even human freedom is somehow both genuine and in all respects held in existence by God, whose touch does not corrupt our integrity but enhances it all ways and always. "But where sin increased, grace abounded all the more" (Rm 5: 20). It is never a choice of all freedom or all grace, but always fully freedom and fully grace. Admittedly we cannot do this in our world, and we do not understand in any full measure how God in God's world can have his cake and eat it too.

We and all other creatures have existence. God is existence. God is his infinite own existence in which is hidden our own. God's essence is his existence, and his existence is his essence. God is a verb and not a noun. God IS, and whatever else is, IS because God totally IS.

If God is everything, i.e., if God is infinite, then how can anything be something? If God is everything, there seems to be no room for anything else not part of "everything." How does God withdraw? How can God create outside himself, yet never outside of everything. The mystery of God is encountered not only in the resurrection of the dead "in the ending" but also in "Let there be light," spoken "in the beginning." Logically we cannot be, yet in God's infinite transcendence here we are, outside God and yet still within God, who is more us that we ourselves. We are no part of God yet altogether of God, by God, and with God, who is One and yet creates Many, wonder of creation, logically impossible and providentially adorable.

Germane to God's infinity, I want to say "I am you." You will say: "no, you are not." So a drop of ocean water might say to other drops, but water seeks the sea and there is only one ocean, though given many names and artificial borders. An ice cube may well claim it is not part of the ocean. After all, it has hard frozen borders, but the ice cube is only water and seeks a return to sea level whenever possible. Boundaries are none. I am you in some mystical but true sense, and you are me. We are profoundly linked, which is why compassion is our natural land, and joy together our ultimate home. There are no boundaries in the created life of God we share, except those we make out of our fear and greed. The butterfly flaps its wings in Brazil and eventually there is a typhoon in Japan. There is only one world climate, in which we are all in touch always and everywhere, even though there are "fronts" and demarcations in the weather, yet always weather has no boundaries. We are all in it together. Planet Earth and the People of God. I am you. Your sins impact me and vice versa. Your goodness and charity impacts me, and I touch you in the Communion of Saints. The heart is not the liver, but though we are many parts, we are but one body and one life, the created life of the God of infinite love. I am you, and at the deepest level of our reflection we know that we belong to each other for better or for worse.

Blessed be the God and Father of our Lord Jesus

Christ, who has blessed us in Christ with every spiritual blessing in the heavenly places, just as he chose us in Christ before the foundation of the world to be holy and blameless before him in love. He destined us for adoption as his children through Jesus Christ, according to the good pleasure of his will, to the praise of his glorious grace that he freely bestowed on us in the Beloved. In him we have redemption through his blood, the forgiveness of our trespasses, according to the riches of his grace that he lavished on us. With all wisdom and insight he has make known to us the mystery of his will according to his good pleasure that he set forth in Christ, as a plan for the fullness of time to gather up all things in him, things in heaven and things on earth" (Eph 1: 3-10).

Then the king will say to those at his right hand, "Come, you that are blessed by my Father, inherit the kingdom prepared for you from the foundation of the world; for I was hungry and you gave me food, I was thirsty and you gave me something to drink, I was a stranger and you welcomed me, I was naked and you gave me clothing, I was sick and you took care of me, I was in prison and you visited me." Then the righteous will answer him, "Lord, when was it that we saw you hungry and gave you food, or thirsty and gave you something to drink? And when was it that we saw you a stranger and welcomed you, or naked and gave you clothing? And when was it that we saw you sick or in prison and visited you? And the king will answer them, "Truly, I tell you, just as you did it to one of the least of these who are members of my family, you did it to me" (Mt 25: 34-40).

CHAPTER EIGHT

God Is Never Worried or Frustrated – God Is Father Almighty and Sovereign Providence

God is provident and provides for all his creation in every way needed. That providence may not easily be seen always and everywhere, but it is truly present if God is God. God is never at the mercy of circumstances or human history, whose very existence depends at every moment on God. The ways of the Father Almighty may be mysterious, but their impact prevails always and everywhere. If God was not providential, if his power and love were not sovereign, then God would resemble human parents, at home wringing their hands, impotent to safeguard their children out in the night. Such a disabled God is a God made in our image. Divine Providence is sovereign over all events; it is more than foresight about the future. Providence is a loving hand supporting the future from within. How does God do it, for such providence would seem improbable, if not impossible? Short answer. No one knows, God knows.

The mystery of providence is the flip side of the mystery of creation. In creation we saw the same problem: if God is everything, how can anything be something? Similarly in the mystery of providence: if God is doing everything, how can anybody with human freedom or anything by pure chance be doing something? God, however, did not create a monster, a runaway world now out of God's control. God is not like a human parent who gave life but can only watch in apprehension as its freedom unfolds beyond its purview. God is not in our image. God is not to be cut down to our logic. "Your God is too small," I want to say. God is infinitely resourceful, and we cannot even imagine how. An impotent God who started something that he cannot finish is not worthy of belief. The Pantocrator, the Father Almighty, love that is power and power that is love, is very believable. Divine providence has to be sovereign if God is God and not just a construction of our own limited imagination and understanding.

If there is a theology of history in the Gospels, it may well be seen in the parable of the wheat and the weeds (Mt 13: 24-30). Accordingly, the good farmer creates a good field of grain, into which an enemy sows weeds. The farmer's servants want to pull up the weeds and make things right, but the farmer argues such intervention will uproot the wheat and make matters worse. "Wait," he says, "at harvest time we will separate the good of history from the bad of history, and you will see how the good did prevail."

Our trouble with this story is that we do not know for sure what is wheat and what is weed in our life and in the world's history. A rose is a weed in a wheat field, and a grain of wheat is a weed in a rose garden. How many times have we thought what we wanted or what was good for us turned bad on us, and how many times did what we thought harmful for us and unwanted turn out to be friend and not foe. Wisdom is a hard lesson learned, but we are the better for it. If we say what belongs in our life will enter by divine providence, and what enters somehow belongs equally by divine providence, we might be close to grasping how God is wisely provident. We tend to think that God is one more player in history, but bigger. We tend to think that God is involved in our history as playwright or stage manager, but the truth of the matter is just the opposite. God is not a player in history; all of history is played out in God, which to say played out in divine providence. The whole world is in God's hands, for were it not it would not exist. Events do happen by human freedom, by chance, and by natural laws of every kind. Nothing happens, however, unless God provides, because God is not in the world, the world is in God, whose providence is sovereign, albeit beyond our logic or calculation. Human life is truly benevolent and good, not because we are good or powerful, but because God is good and powerful, and he does have the whole world in his hands, including you and me and everyone else. You may marshal examples to the contrary, but you do not know the whole story to the ending that is just the beginning.

Our prayers of petition amount to this. "O Lord God, take care of this and that, take care of me, take care of us." Divine Providence is divine care. We propose to God just how he might take care of us all and our affairs in this world, but God's answer to our prayer exceeds what we ask for, even if at the moment we do not see any such relief and care. Why can I say this? Two reasons give me hope. God knows what we need better than we do and well before we do, and God loves us and our world in seeming jeopardy more than we do ourselves, even without our asking divine assistance. Our prayers of petition for this and for that could well be reduced to a simple prayer of thankfulness and hopefulness: "O Lord God, I know you are taking care of all this. Thank you so much. What more might I be doing to help"?

> He said to his disciples, "Therefore I tell you, do not worry about your life, what you will eat, or about your body, what you will wear. For life is more than food, and the body more than clothing. Consider the ravens; they neither sow nor reap, they have neither storehouse nor barn, and yet God feeds them. Of how much more value are you than the birds! And can any of you by worrying add a single hour to your span of life? If then you are not able to do so small a thing as that, why do you worry about the rest? Consider the lilies, how they grow; they neither toil nor spin; yet I tell you, even Solomon in all his glory was not clothed like one of these. But if God so clothes the grass of the field, which is alive today and tomorrow is thrown into the oven, how much more will he clothe you -- you of little faith! And do not keep striving for what you are to eat and what

you are to drink, and do not keep worrying. For it is the nations of the world that strive after all these things, and your Father knows that you need them. Instead strive for his kingdom, and these things will be given to you as well.

Do not be afraid, little flock, for it is your Father's good pleasure to give you the kingdom. Sell your possessions and give alms. Make purses for yourselves that do not wear out, an unfailing treasure in heaven, where no thief comes near and no moth destroy. For where your treasure is, there your heart will be also" (Lk 12: 22-34).

We know that all things work together for good for those who love God, who are called according to his purpose (Rm 8: 28).

CHAPTER NINE

God Is Never Changing or Wavering – God Is Ever Faithful

God is a promise-keeper. God's Covenant with Israel was given once and for all, forever and never to be repealed, for better or for worse, a "love that does not alter when it alteration finds." If humanity was ever loved by God, if we were ever loved by God, then we are loved forever. St. Paul was convinced that God would not let the Hebrew people miss out on the "New Covenant," inaugurated in the life and death of Jesus Christ, because Paul knew God does not withdraw his love no matter the hesitation of his beloved people ever called into everlasting covenant with God. "Can a woman forget her suckling child, that she should not have compassion on the son of her womb? Yea, they may forget, yet will I not forget thee.

Behold, I have graven thee upon the palms of my hands" (Is. 49:15-16). God is never wavering in love or loyalty to those he has given his love, and in Jesus we believe his love given to all of us. God's promises endure forever and suffer no change. Peter was beloved by Jesus, and though he denied him three times at the time of his passion and death, Jesus came to Peter and the disciples, who had run away from Calvary, and he offers Peter a renewal of their bond of love. "Peter, do you love me?" Three times Jesus asks him the same question, and Peter answers despite his past infidelity, "you know that I do." Jesus concludes: "Then feed my sheep," and Peter is established again in the covenant with the Lord Jesus, a covenant and a love that nothing can rupture.

Francis Thompson's poem, "The Hound of Heaven," captures so well the persistent and ineluctable pursuit that God entails on God's beloved. What God wants God will achieve, for his pursuit is everlasting and his resources without end. You can run from God but you cannot hide. He does not weary, and in the end, God will hold us all in his arms. Such is our hope, and it is not an unfounded hope. The parable of the Prodigal Son captures the same faithful and never tiring love. In that story the Father does not pursue his wayward son, but awaits every day his return, which one suspects the Father anticipates as inevitable because of the strength of his love for his son. The elder son is resentful of the ample mercy and celebration given his younger brother, and he is resentful of his father whom he thinks takes his labors for granted. But the Father loves both of his sons, and goes out to his elder and angry son and reassures him that "everything I have is yours," but we had to celebrate "because this brother of yours was dead and has come to life; he was lost and has been found" (Luke 15: 32).

Both sons misunderstood their father's love for them. The younger son thought that he had forever lost his father's love by his bad behavior, and the elder son thought that he had forever gained his father's love by his good behavior. Both sons are wrong. They are loved by their father because they are his sons, and they are loved forever because they are his sons forever. They neither lose their father's love by whatever they do, nor gain it by whatever they do. The father loved them before they were born and will love them all through this earthly life until they are born from the womb of this world into eternal life. And then, when the world "in the ending" has been born into the Kingdom of God in heaven, we shall know that faithful and everlasting love of God, "the love that moves the sun and the others stars" (Dante's last line of the Divine Comedy). That love makes the world "in the beginning" and loves it "in the ending." On the last evening of his life on earth, Jesus "having loved his own which were in the world, he loved them unto the end" (Jn 13:1).

There was a man who had two sons. The younger of them said to his father, "Father, give me the share of the property that will belong to me." So he divided his property between them. A few days later the younger son gathered all he had and traveled to a distant country, and there he squandered his property in dissolute living. When he has spent everything, a severe famine took place throughout that country, and he began to be in need. So he went and hired himself out to one of the citizens of that country, who sent him to his fields to feed the pigs. He would have gladly have filled himself with the pods that the pigs were eating; and no one gave him anything. But when he came to himself he said. "How many of my father's hired hands have bread enough and to spare, but here I am dying of hunger! I will get up and go to my father, and I will say to him, 'Father, I have sinned against heaven and before you; I am no longer worthy to be called your son; treat me like one of your hired hands.'" So he set off and went to his father. But while he was still far off, his father saw him and was filled with compassion; he ran and put his arms around him and kissed him. Then the son said to him, "Father, I have sinned against heaven and before you; I am no longer worthy to be called your son." But the Father said to his slaves, "Quickly, bring out a robe – the best one – and put it on him; put a ring on his finger and sandals on his feet. And get the fatted calf and kill it, and let us eat and celebrate; for this son of mine was dead and is alive again; he was lost and is found!" And they began to celebrate.

Now his elder son was in the field; and when he came and approached the house, he heard music and dancing. He called one of the slaves and asked what was going on. He replied, "Your brother has come, and your father has killed the fatted calf, because he has got him back safe and sound." Then he became angry and refused to go in. His father came out and began to plead with him. But he answered his father, "Listen! For all these years I have been working like a slave for you, and I have never disobeyed your command; yet you have never given me even a young goat so that I might celebrate with my friends. But when this son of yours came back, who has devoured your property with prostitutes, you killed the fatted calf for him!" Then the father said to him, "Son, you are always with me, and all that is mine is yours. But we had to celebrate and rejoice, because this brother of yours was dead and has come to life; he was lost and has been found" (Lk 15: 11-32).

I fled Him, down the nights and down the days;
   I fled Him, down the arches of the years;
I fled Him, down the labyrinthine ways
   Of my own mind; and in the midst of tears
I hid from Him, and under running laughter.
           Up vistaed hopes I sped;
           And shot precipitated,
Adown Titanic glooms of chasmed fears,
   From those strong Feet that followed, followed after.
           But with unhurrying chase,
           And unperturbed pace,
Deliberate speed, majestic instancy,
           They beat – a Voice beat
           More instant than the Feet –
"All things betray thee, who betrayest Me."

        Francis Thompson
        "The Hound of Heaven" (first stanza)

CHAPTER TEN

God Is Never Judgmental or Punitive – God Is Ever Merciful

If God is infinitely merciful and perennially (seventy times seven) forgiving, do we need to worry with such a God that we might find ourselves across the sea in hell? I suppose we have to say that such a dire outcome is possible, though we need not believe it is probable for anyone. Consider the "good thief" on the cross. "This day you will be with me in paradise," says Jesus (Lk 23: 43). Of the other thief, the "bad thief," he may have had a change of heart when he had gotten out what he had to say when we were not listening. God alone knows.

Hell is a hellish place, no doubt, but let us not turn God into a torturer who takes sadistic pleasure in pain. Dante's "Inferno" is a work of imagination. Fire and brimstone together with demon torture is all part and parcel of apocalyptic metaphorical literature popular in ancient times, and more recently in private revelations that no one need credit as Gospel truth. Jesus speaks here and there in the Gospels in apocalyptic terms. He was in his rhetoric a product of his culture and time. We need not conclude that we are given a videotape of the reality of separation from God for all eternity, which is the essence of any hell. To be apart from all that is good, true, and beautiful suggests no further punishment could be conceived or needed.

God does not have mercy. God is mercy. There is nothing in God but mercy and all the virtues, including justice and love. God is infinite perfection that we cannot imagine. Our distortion of God makes God in some depictions very judgmental, waiting to catch human beings in their sins and then quick to punish them with everlasting torment should they unrepentant or untimely die. That punitive and suspicious quality attributed to God undeservedly all too often comes from our own behavior as human beings that we project onto God. God is not mean or harsh like us. God does not demand a "pound of flesh" for our trespasses and our debts. God is not made in our image; we are made in God's image and often distort it with our ungodly cruelty. We may think we are acting like God, because the Sacred Scriptures do depict at times an angry and threatening God whose vengeance is to be feared (see Mt 25). Alas, do remember that the Scriptures were written by human authors to whom the Word of God came not as dictation but as inspiration and for whom the language and culture of their time controlled the kind of writing about God that the writers would have at their command. As all of us, they are children of their age. "Eye for an eye and tooth for a tooth" was common practice, and when the Bible says of God "vengeance is mine, says the Lord" (Rm 12: 19), our approach is to soften our vengeance and revenge and not to increase what is already in the human heart, much less project our hard heart and the brutality of our circumstances and culture upon God. A much more adequate picture of God is given us in Jesus, who said to the woman caught in adultery and about to be brutally stoned to death by an angry mob of men from whom Jesus saves her: "neither do I condemn thee, but go and sin no more" (Jn 8: 11).

However, you will say, "what about Judgment Day and the separation of the goats and the sheep, the former to everlasting torment and the latter to everlasting happiness"? You can, of course, cherry-pick sentences in the Bible to support most anything. Once again I assume the evangelist was a child of his culture, and the world of Israel at the time of Jesus was harsh as befits a land often without police, law courts, or any justice but the ruler's judgment or the crowd's reaction. That version of justice was often the only after-life deterrent that good people could offer.

Christians profess in the Creed that Jesus will come again to "judge the living and dead." What kinds of judgment should we be talking about? Three kinds of judgment emerge upon reflection. (1) Self-judgment might be how God judges us, letting us see ourselves as we are and not as we imagine, and we ourselves make the judgment call on that basis. Judgment on the last day will be a revelation. Nothing further need be said. (2) Bench judgment is what all of us have experienced with teachers who grade us, parents who punish us, courts of law that decide our guilt or innocence. Bench judgment can be wrong, but God is never wrong. God is not prejudiced (pre-judge). God is not vindictive. God is never unfair, nor does God ever fail to take into consideration all of the extenuating circumstances of our life from the moment of our conception. God is the bench judge who knows all of the evidence top to bottom, and who is favorably disposed to each and every one of us no matter what we have or have not done. Only God knows the whole story, and one suspects if we knew the whole story we would be so much less punitive and much more merciful. We would then be eager to apply remedial love and healing resources from the first moments the offender's moral compass began to go south. "There but for the grace of God go I" speaks of a merciful compassion in human beings that is but the weak image of the all-merciful and compassionate heart of God, what Christians know as the "Sacred Heart of Jesus," who died for each one of us out of his love for us and not out of his anger with us. (3) Judgment might be understood as a conclusion: "it is finished" (Jn 19: 30). An artist judges a painting complete, an author judges the novel is ended, God judges the earth and its history and finds that his will to save us all has been completed. "For God so loved the world that he gave his only Son, so that everyone who believes in him may not perish but may have eternal life" (Jn 3:16). Our computers can justify the margins, and suddenly they all are lined up even-steven. God can justify the world in God's sovereign providence. God can lift every valley and make every mountain and hill low (Is 40: 4). Only God writes straight with crooked lines, and even sin can serve the purposes of God whose grace abounds the more where sin seems to abound.

I love the onion-lady story in Dostoievsky's *Brothers Karamazov*. Told briefly it goes like this. St. Peter, guardian of the gates of heaven and hell, notices a poor lady in the fires of hell and has pity for her and wonders if maybe he misjudged her. He asks her did she not ever do one good thing in her life, however small? She ponders and finally offers this one example. She once gave a rotten onion to a poor beggar. "That's enough," says St. Peter. He lowers down the rotten onion into hell, and the woman grabs hold and she begins to be lifted out of hell. But then, she looks down and sees someone holding onto her ankles and a chain of people holding on to each other. The onion does not break; they are all coming out of hell. Only then, only when the woman kicks off the chain of people clinging to her for salvation, does the rotten onion break.

I hear you say: "and what about Hell? Hell has to be a possibility, because if we can say "yes" to God, it must be possible to say "no." That hell exists is thus a Christian doctrine, but the Church has never said it knows there are many people in hell, or any particular villain in hell, or indeed, even any one person. We do not know. Consider this analogy. We know human beings can run the four-minute mile. We know they cannot run the four-second mile and never will be able to. We could argue that it is possible for a human being to run the three-minute mile, but no one may ever do it. Why? Because so many factors would have to come together and they may never do so. The runner would have to have the ideal constitution and muscle formation, the best coaching, motivation to a high degree, leisure and strength for years of dedication and long training, the right shoes, the right track, the right weather, the right competition to pace him, and much more. It is possible, but it may never happen. Similarly it may be possible to outsmart or outrun the "hound of heaven," the merciful God who is infinitely resourceful. But, "lots of luck" is what I want to say. It may be possible to say "no" to God, but it is not probable if God is engaged in our world with the resourcefulness of infinite power, love, and grace. The "hound of heaven" is going to dog your footsteps with a cunning stamina far beyond your own stamina. I used to tell my students that they would find it difficult, but not impossible, to flunk my course. I would pursue them if they were absent or failed a test. Are they drinking or drugging, or depressed? Have they lost a boy/girl friend, death of a parent, or a family in divorce? Are they in the wrong course level without adequate prior learning? Whatever the cause, there are remedies at hand short of failure. The Dean can authorize an incomplete grade or pull a student from a course with no penalty. But, since I do not love my students as much as God loves each one of us, and the Dean, unlike God, does not have infinite resources, a student of mine can manage to fail. Bottom line, we do know God is infinitely resourceful with his grace and power and wishes to save us all. You may say I am too optimistic, but I would say you are not hopeful enough. God is infinite loving, and his love is his mercy and his mercy is his love.

If you then say: "well if there is that kind of mercy in the world, let us all pile on with the sinful life and get away with murder." But, sin is misery, even though our culture misleads us otherwise. We are fooled by the "Prince of lies." Sin has made no one happy or fulfilled. The first victim of any sin or crime is the sinner, and the most damage in a spiritual way is never to the victim, but always to the sinner. You have to be blind, or stupid and blind, to be a sinner once the fog of delusion has been lifted by the grace of God or the passage of time.

"It ain't fair," I can hear someone say. But the Catholic notion of Purgatory is what allows the hope of universal salvation to be fair. Purgatory properly understood is not a sadistic place of fire and retribution. It is moral and spiritual re-habilitation. The people in Purgatory want to stop smoking and lose weight. They want to go through the agonies of diet and exercise. They want to be at last clean and lean. They want what God wants, not revenge but salvation, not punishment but compassion. They want not the punitive justice of our criminal system on earth, but the restorative justice of the Kingdom of God in heaven. That is not unfair. That is not a free pass. Jesus died for us so that every sin will be redeemed and at a cost of much effort toward the total conversion of life that was not accomplished in this our earthly sojourn. Granted it is a second chance, but is this not what it is all about with the coming of Jesus on earth? Adam and Eve are to be given a second chance. Regaining Paradise is offered them. Why do we want to make God stingy and unwilling to give the sinner yet another chance? No one fails in Purgatory, because they have seen their sins and have known the mercy of God. We are all too often like the workers in the vineyard who resent the same pay for the folks who worked but an hour and those who worked all the day long. The vineyard owner puts it well: "Am I not allowed to do what I choose with what belongs to me? Or are you envious because I am generous" (Mt 20: 15).

If the reader is still uncertain and wonders how all the talk of judgment and punishment in the Bible and in Church Tradition is to be accounted for, let me try a short summation. In the centuries when there was no sheriff in most times and places and no rule of law and enforcement, the only remedy for people seeking justice and peace was an emphasis on the sheriff in heaven and the judgment court and the punishments of the afterlife. To some extent those threats taken to heart by a somewhat credulous people hopefully reduced rape, pillage, and plunder in a brutal world. Today we do have increasing justice in this world, as imperfect as it may still be. We no longer need God to be punitive, if judgment is now understood as God opening our eyes so that we see who we are and what we have done. We will judge ourselves. The truth will stare us in the face. As a professor of composition, I used to sit a student down and read back to them their essay very slowly with pregnant pauses. Often nothing more needed to be said. They saw and heard where they went wrong. Similarly, God does not need to punish anyone. Sin is its own punishment, and in that merciless exposure to the truth about ourselves we will see what self-isolation we have created, so much that we were given and wasted, and what we have done to our self, others, and to our world. There will be no greater punishment needed or possible. And if one believes in a Purgatory after death, there may yet be hope for us sinners.

It may be helpful to remember that the "Death Penalty" is a human verdict tinged with out vengeance. A "Life Sentence" without chance of parole is also a human sentencing, and solitary confinement is a humanly designed infliction. Let us not project our image of punishment and our impotence in the face of injustice upon God, who is ever merciful and infinitely resourceful with regard to any and all evil and injustice.

> Early in the morning he came again to the temple. All the people came to him and he sat down and began to teach them. The scribes and the Pharisees brought a woman who had been caught in adultery; and making her stand before all of them, they said to him, "Teacher, this woman was caught in the very act of committing adultery. Now in the law Moses commanded us to stone such women. Now what do you say"? They said this to test him so that they might have some charge to bring against him. Jesus bent down and wrote with his finger on the ground. When they kept on questioning him, he straightened up and said to them. "Let anyone among you who is without sin be the first to throw a stone at her." And once again he bent down and wrote on the

ground. When they heard it, they went away, one by one, beginning with the elders; and Jesus was left alone with the woman standing before him. Jesus straightened up and said to her. "Woman, where are they? Has no one condemned you?" She said, "No one sir." And Jesus said, "Neither do I condemn you. Go your way, and from now on do not sin again" (Jn 8: 2-11).

One of the Pharisees asked Jesus to eat with him, and he went into the Pharisee's house and took his place at table. And a woman in the city, who was a sinner, having learned that he was eating in the Pharisee's house, brought an alabaster jar of ointment. She stood behind him at his feet weeping, and began to bathe his feet with her tears and to dry them with her hair. Then she continued kissing his feet and anointing them with the ointment. Now when the Pharisee who had invited him saw it, he said to himself, "If this man were a prophet, he would have known who and what kind of woman this is who is touching him – that she is a sinner." Jesus spoke up and said to him, "Simon, I have something to say to you." "Teacher," he replied, "Speak." "A certain creditor had two debtors; one owed five hundred denarii, and the other fifty. When they could not pay, he canceled the debt for both of them. Now which of them will love him more?" Simon answered, "I suppose the one for whom he canceled the greater debt." And Jesus said to him, "You have judged rightly." Then turning toward the woman he said to Simon, "Do you see this woman? I entered your house; you gave me no water for my feet, but she has bathed my feet with her tears and dried them with her hair. You gave me no kiss but from the time I came in she has not stopped kissing my feet. You did not anoint my head with oil, but she has anointed my feet with ointment. Therefore, I tell you, her sins, which were many, have been forgiven; hence she has shown great love. But the one to whom little is forgiven loves little." Then he said to her, "Your sins are forgiven." But those who were at the table with him began to say among themselves, "Who is this who even forgives sins?" And he said to the woman, "Your faith has saved you; go in peace" (Lk 7: 36-50).

CHAPTER ELEVEN

God Is Not Heartless
– God Is Love and Nothing Less

One might object. You say God is so loving. You say God is love. You say God is sovereign and his providence blankets all that happens in this world. Nothing is unknown or unforeseen to God who stands in an eternal now, knowing the future and the past, all of time in the Eternal Moment. You say God finds existence in all its apparent chaos glorious and "very good." So, one might ask, why so much human suffering and evolutionary predation of every kind? Either God does not care, as you claim he does, or God cannot intervene, having made a world with laws of nature God will not contravene.

Suppose I say God could run the world with miracles, cure the sick with "but only speak the word and my servant will be healed" (Mt 8: 8). Suppose God could feed you without any effort on your part, are you sure you would not prefer to raise your own food, bake your own bread, and set your own table? Do we not stand in for God in the works of mercy in this world? Are not hospitals but God's mercy in our hands? But, you say, you use the victims of illness as subjects for my practice of virtue. Yes and No. If God gave us everything without any effort on our part, would we not feel like a "kept woman," indebted for everything we have, never knowing or having it be known that we did it all for love rather than that we just struck a bargain to be spared the responsibility of real freedom and real risks, a world of real surprises, a world that need not make sense to us here and now, but only then and there before Him.

The answer to the suffering of Job is not given to Job or to us. After the *Book of Job*, God does not speak again in the Bible until he says all in his Word, the one Word, made flesh and saying everything. God says in Jesus not words of explanation, but deeds of solidarity and confirmation of this world. God promises to provide for life and to console us in our suffering. Jesus worked miracles to manifest God's will to relieve suffering, but he did not opt for a world of divine miracles. He left us to be his hands and his heart on earth. He asks us to trust in his wisdom and in his love, and as far as the sufferings of this life that baffle us for their relief, Jesus said only this: "I will walk through it with you." The cross is not a bucket of answers, but a bucket of blood given for us to know as only in this way could we know, how much God loves us and hopes we can wait yet a bit longer to know all about why this world and not another, were we God, which we are not, thank God! In the end "God will wipe away every tear from their eyes" (Rev 7:7).

I do not want to underestimate the horrors of human suffering, especially I do not wish to push aside the enormous scandal of man's inhumanity to man. Hegel said understandably, "history is a butcher's bench." We know that human history consists only of what we kept some kind of record. Lost to memory and recorded history remain the incalculable incidents of human pain and tragedy over the centuries of human existence on planet earth. Christians believe Jesus is God with us, God made flesh among us, who was born and died like we do. His crucifixion and resurrection give the only answer to the problem of suffering that has a chance of reconciling the human heart to suffering. He did not give us an explanation, but God gave us a demonstration. In your own human flesh I will walk through with you all the agonies of this world. In my own body I will capsulize your lives, one and all, and take them all with me into a resurrected and eternal life with God the Father of all mysteries and hidden blessings. I will remember it all. No tear will be wasted, no suffering unnoticed, no pain not assuaged. If that divine response to human suffering does not bolster belief that God is with us in love, then, dear reader, I have lost you on this score.

As the Father has loved me, so I have loved you; abide in my love. If you keep my commandments, you will abide in my love, just as I have kept my Father's commandments and abide in his love. I have said these things to you so that my joy may be in you, and that your joy may be complete. This is my commandment, that you love one another as I have loved you. No one has greater love than this, to lay down one's life for one's friends. You are my friends if you do what I command you. I do not call you servants any longer, because the servant does not know what the master is doing; but I have called you friends, because I have made known to you everything that I have heard from my Father. You did not choose me but I chose you. And I appointed you to go and bear fruit, fruit that will last, so that the Father will give you whatever you ask him in my name. I am giving you these commands so that you may love one another (Jn 15: 9-17).

If I speak in the tongues of mortals and angels, but do not have love, I am a noisy gong or a clanging cymbal. And if I have prophetic powers, and understand all mysteries and all knowledge, and if I have all faith, so as to remove mountains, but do not have love, I am nothing. If I give away all my possessions, and if I hand over my body so that I may boast, but do not have love, I gain nothing. Love is patient; love is kind; love is not envious or boastful or arrogant or rude. It does not insist on its own way; it is not irritable or resentful; it does not rejoice in wrongdoing, but rejoices in the truth. It bears all things, believes all things; hopes all things, endures all things. Love never ends" (1 Cor 13: 1-8).

Beloved, let us love one another, because love is from God; everyone who loves is born of God and knows God, for God is love. God's love was revealed among us in this way: God sent his only Son into the world so that we might live through him. In this is love, not that we loved God but that he loved us and sent his Son to be the atoning sacrifice for our sins. Beloved, since God loved us so much, we also ought to love one another. No one has ever seen God; if we love one another, God lives in us, and his love is perfected in us (1 Jn 4: 7-12).

CHAPTER TWELVE

In God There Is No Darkness – God Is Light and Truth

GOD IS LIGHT, and in him there is no darkness. "In your [God's] light, we see light" (Ps 36: 9). With our human eyes we do not see light in and of itself; we see light reflected. We see a derived light. Jesus said he was "the light of the world" (Jn 8: 12). In the beginning God said "Let there be light" (Gn 1: 3). When we understand something we often say, "now I see." Seeing and understanding go together, and we see with our mind as with our eyes. To see the truth of anything is to stand in the light and not in the darkness of error or ignorance. "If your eye is healthy, your whole body will be full of light" (Mt 6: 22)). The truth is clear and full of light. Jesus asked Bartimaeus, the blind man on the road to Jericho, what he wanted. He said to Jesus what all of us with our minds set on the truth want to say: "Let me see" (Mk 10: 51). Written in a moment of darkness, Cardinal Newman tells of the human desire to be guided by God's light shining in our darkness. His well known prayer comes to mind:

Lead kindly light,
Amid the encircling gloom.
Lead Thou me on!
The night is dark
And I am far from home —
Lead Thou me on!
Keep Thou my feet;
I do not ask to see
The distant scene —
One step enough for me.

Sinfulness is darkness. Sin makes no sense; sin is non-sense. There is no understanding possible when the light has been extinguished. Sin is willful. I want what I want because I want it, and I want it now. It makes no sense to contradict the truth and hope for an outcome that is not opaque. If you want to be happy, and I say then take the road to virtue and love, and you say I want to take the road of vice and selfishness, then I will say you can't get there from here. Imagine someone in South Bend who wants to go to Chicago and the train waiting in the station is going to Chicago, and you get on the train going in the opposite direction to Cleveland. It makes no sense; such a decision is nonsense. I say, "You are getting on the wrong train, and it will not take you in the right direction," and you say "I want to get on the train to Cleveland, and I am going to do what I want, come what may." With that attitude, predictably, misery will come your way. Sin is nonsense and it leads to misery.

Conversion of life is the remedy for sin. We have to choose to live in the light. We have to pursue the truth, recognize it, and live by it. Conversion is coming into the light. The man who was blind from birth and healed by Jesus knows the radical change in his life: "One thing I do know, that though I was blind now I see" (Jn 9: 25). Consider this analogy. All diets work and you will lose weight. Some diets might be more nutritious and some might leave one less hungry and more likely to succeed. But all diets that reduce considerably caloric intake over a period of time will lead to a weight loss. The problem is that most people, when the dieting is over, go back to old ways and regain the weight lost and sometimes more in addition. What has to happen to lose weight for good is this. We have to see food in a true light. We have to recognize that food is not a solution for our emotional needs or any other lack in our life. We have to see food in a different light and recognize the truth about what food can and cannot do in our life. It cannot solve our problems. It can provide health and an opportunity to share companionship with others at table. Conversion is to see with new eyes. Sin is not the truth. Healthy life is to see with new eyes. Overeating is not the truth. It is again like getting on the train to Cleveland when you really wanted to go to Chicago. It made no sense. It was nonsense. It had no light. It was darkness.

> They came to Jericho. As he [Jesus] and his disciples and a large crowd were leaving Jericho, Bartimaeus, son of Timaeus, a blind beggar, was sitting by the roadside. When he heard that it was Jesus of Nazareth, he began to shout out and say, "Jesus, Son of David, have mercy on me"! Many sternly ordered him to be quiet, but he cried out even more loudly. "Son of David, have mercy on me"! Jesus stood still and said, "Call him here."

And they called the blind man, saying to him. "Take heart; get up, he is calling you." So throwing off his cloak, he sprang up and came to Jesus. Then Jesus said to him, "What do you want me to do for you"? The blind man said to him, "My teacher, let me see again." Jesus said to him, "Go; your faith has made you well." Immediately he regained his sight and followed him on the way (Mk 10: 46-52).

By the tender mercy of our God, the dawn from on high will break upon us,

To give light to those who sit in darkness and the shadow of death,

To guide our feet into the way of peace.

(Lk 1: 78-79)

CHAPTER THIRTEEN

God Is Not the God of the Dead – God Is God of the Living

Jesus came to save the world and to ensure that we would have life and have it more abundantly. Jesus said he was the way (the way of love, the way of the cross as self-donation) the truth (the light of the world) and the life (the life that death cannot take away). Of the God of Abraham, Isaac, and Jacob, Jesus proclaimed: "Now he is God not of the dead, but of the living; for to him all of them are alive" (Lk 20:38).

Tolkien's masterful novel, *Lord of the Rings*, introduces the reader to the hobbits -- small, vulnerable, and loveable creatures of intelligence that remind one of good

and simple human beings. They live in a dark and dangerous world, and their heroic deeds have an impact for good
or evil beyond calculation. The miracle is not to walk on
water or fly through the air. The miracle is to walk on the
earth. The whole purpose of human life may just be the
quest to become human, all that a human being can be
in imagination and goodness, all that a human being can
be in care and tenderness. Human beings are so little in
the scheme and scale of the cosmos, and yet only human
beings, as far as we know, do appreciate the universe and
are invited to take responsibility for the outcome of its
human history. Being conscious changes everything. We
know, and we know that we know, and we know that we
know that we know. And we know when we do not know,
at least we hope we do. And our peril often is that we do
not know what we do not know, a circumstance that can
lead to disaster.

Human life is subject to comedy and to tragedy, to a
happy ending and an unhappy ending. When Prospero
asks Ariel, the spritely spirit in Shakespeare's "Tempest,"
whether or not he should forgive his enemies, he replies:
"I would, were I human." One thinks of the plight of the
character called Radar in the "Star Trek" drama. More
than humanly intelligent, human in appearance and task

responsibility, Radar cannot generate human emotion and commitment. To be a human being is to be spiritually alive. We are animated body and inspirited flesh. We are incarnate spirit and infleshed soul. Conscious of being conscious and living with a moral conscience, human beings have one foot on earth and one foot in the heavens. We span the world. We are not the center of the universe, but we are a center of the universe, because our mind can comprehend what we see and understand and in ever greater concentration. So little in body and mind, yet we can be and do so much.

Fully a third of the gospels tell of Jesus healing the human body and mind. In particular, he gives sight to the blind. He raises the dead. He honors the body and intends to show that God gave human beings life and wishes that life to flourish. There is to be "the resurrection of the body and life everlasting." God is a God of the living. He does not preside over a giant cemetery of ages past. We shall see each other again. When a child is born, a treasure of great price has been given us, for only human beings live forever. Monuments of granite will become dust from the erosion of wind and rain, given enough time. Only human beings have the hope of everlasting life, and life in the company of the God of life itself, the God who does not have life but is life. We shall share God's life and live forever in God's presence. Such is the hope of Christians and such is the hope of many others who also believe in God. "In him we move, and live, and have our being" (Acts 17: 28).

We know we are born to die. We are mortal and our bodies will age beyond repair. Death need not be a dead end, however. Death can be a beginning of a new life. The child is born from its mother's womb into this vast and glorious world far surpassing life in the womb. Similarly, persons who believe in eternal life with God believe they are born again from out of the womb of this body that is the world. When we die we are going to our wedding with the God we have loved within and behind all the other loves of our life in this world. We do not go to our funeral. We go to our wedding; our friends and family attend us at our funeral. In the film, "Babette's Feast," we encounter the mystery of eternal life in words of great beauty.

> Mercy and Truth have met together. Righteousness and Bliss shall kiss one another. We, in our weakness and shortsightedness believe we must make choices in this life. We tremble at the risks we take. But no! How important is our choice? There comes a time when our eyes are open, and we come to realize that mercy is infinite. We need only await it with confidence and

receive it in gratitude. Mercy imposes no conditions. And lo! Everything we have chosen has been granted to us, and everything we have rejected has also been granted. Yes, we even get back what we rejected. For Mercy and Truth have met together. Righteousness and Bliss shall kiss one another.

(From the film, "Babette's Feast," which is an adaption of the short written by Karen Dinesen, a.k.a. Karen Blixen).

Some Sadducees, those who say there is no resurrection, came to him and asked him a question, "Teacher, Moses wrote for us that if a man's brother dies, leaving a wife but no children, the man shall marry the widow and raise up children for his brother. Now there were seven brothers; the first married, and died childless; then the second and the third married her, and so in the same way all seven died childless. Finally the woman also died. In the resurrection, therefore, whose wife will the woman be? For the seven had married her"? Jesus said to them, "Those who belong to this age marry and are given in marriage; but those who are considered worthy of a place in that age and in the resurrection from the dead neither marry nor are given in marriage. Indeed they cannot die anymore, because they are like angels and are children of God, being children of the resurrection. And the fact that the dead are raised

Moses himself showed, in the story about the bush [the burning bush in Exodus] where he speaks of the Lord as the God of Abraham, the God of Isaac, and the God of Jacob. Now he is God not of the dead, but of the living; for to him all of them are alive." (Lk 20: 27-38))

But Mary stood weeping outside the tomb. As she wept, she bent over to look into the tomb; and she saw two angels in white, sitting where the body of Jesus had been lying, one at the head and the other at the feet. They said to her, "Woman, why are you weeping"? She said to them, "They have taken away my Lord, and I do not know where they have laid him." When she had said this she turned around and saw Jesus standing there, but she did not know that it was Jesus. Jesus said to her, "Woman, why are you weeping? Whom are you looking for"? Supposing him to be the gardener she said to him. "Sir, if you have carried him away, tell me where you have laid him, and I will take him away." Jesus said to her, "Mary!" She turned and said to him in Hebrew, "Rabbouni!" (which means Teacher). Jesus said to her, "Do not hold on to me, because I have not yet ascended to the Father. But go to my brothers and say to them, 'I am ascending to my Father and your Father, to my God and your God'" (Jn 20: 11-17).

CHAPTER FOURTEEN

No One Has Seen God
– God Is Revealed in Jesus of Nazareth

No one has seen God because God has no body to be seen. Mystics have claimed some kind of union with God, but God is not available to human eyesight, not because God chooses to be hidden away from us, but because there is nothing for the human eye to gaze upon. God is spirit, and as such works in our world as spirit. God illumines our minds and enkindles our hearts.

Jesus, however, is the face of God made human, and he tells his disciple, Philip, that whoever sees Jesus sees the Father: "Philip said to him, 'Lord, show us the Father, and we will be satisfied.' Jesus said to him, 'Have I been with you all this time, Philip, and you still do not know me? Whoever has seen me has seen the Father. How can you say, "Show us the Father"? Do you not believe that I am in the Father and the Father is in me? The words that I say to you I do not speak on my own; but the Father who dwells in me does his works. Believe me that I am in the Father and the Father is in me; but if you do not, then believe because of the works themselves'" (Jn 14: 8-11).

One could argue that God could conceal himself from being seen in any sense of the word "seen," if God so chose. The revelation of God is a freely chosen gift of God to disclose himself to his created human beings, who have no demand for "revelation" that they could justify. God need not reveal himself. The mystery of Jesus becomes the disclosure of God to the eyes of faith. Yet we know more of God than we can say: "No one has ever seen God; if we love one another God lives in us, and his love is perfected in us" (1 Jn 4: 12).

When we see someone or something we somehow take that vision into our self. We are united to what we see. We take the person into our self. To gaze on someone is somehow to have access to that person, even on the inside. The eyes are the windows of the soul, and to look into someone's eyes can be an invasive intimacy. Native Americans were often opposed to having their photograph taken, because they feared something of them was taken away from them. The bride is veiled, for the revelation of who she is and the beauty of her face belongs alone to the husband who loves her and not to a curious crowd. Only the bridegroom may lift the veil. We reveal our self to the one we love.

Because God loves us, he would have us see his face, but not in a way to overwhelm our eyes, but in a way that takes into account that we can see most deeply into another human face. Hence the face of Jesus, the life of Jesus, both a glimpse into the face of God and how, were God human, God would live and love and lay down his life for his friends. What more could God do for us? How else more wonderfully could God speak with human beings? Nothing comes close to such communing with us, not as in a masquerade, but enfleshed as one of us, and not for a day, a year, or a momentary apparition, but human altogether like us forever more. We were created in the image of God. In Jesus that image is so perfectly, substantially, and totally embodied that Jesus reveals the Father – "God from God, Light from Light, true God from true God," consubstantial, the Word of God made flesh and dwelt among us.

He is the image of the invisible God, the firstborn
of all creation; for in him all things in heaven and on
earth were created, things visible and invisible, whether
thrones or dominions or rulers or powers – all things
have been created through him and for him. He himself
is before all things, and in him all things hold together.
He is head of the body, the church; he is the beginning,
the firstborn from the dead, so that he might come to
have first place in everything. For in him all the fullness
of God was pleased to dwell. And through him God
was pleased to reconcile to himself all things, whether
on earth or in heaven, by making peace through the
blood of his cross (Col 1: 15-20).

CHAPTER FIFTEEN

The Eucharist Is Not Embarrassing – The Eucharist Is Only Misunderstood

"Eat my body and drink my blood" are familiar words that may find their way into the rhetoric of Eucharistic hymns, but taken literally they leave us aghast. The Eucharist is not about pain, blood, nor sacrifice as bodily destruction, nor about the recipient of the bread and wine entering into something unmentionable. The Eucharist is a meal and it is a sacrifice, but the meal is unlike any other and so is the un-bloody sacrifice.

Here is the problem. Human beings want nothing more in their heart of hearts than to give their life for those they love. We spend ourselves on what we love. "For where your treasure is, there your heart will be also" (Lk 12: 34). Self-donation is at the heart of human beings and at the heart of the Eucharist. It is also at the heart of the bloody sacrifice of animals in the religious rituals of antiquity. We want to give our life; we want to recognize with our lives the God who gave us our lives, but we do not think God wants us to open a vein and bleed out for God's sake. So, we take a symbol of ourselves, an animal of sacrifice, whose life we do bleed out as a representation of our moral intent to give our life over completely to God. Jesus gave himself to us as bread at the Last Supper. Bread supports our life. He gave himself to us as bread so that we might live. His life was to become our life. In the crucifixion Jesus actually sheds his blood, but that is not where the inner action resides. The inner intent is to lay down his life for us and not just to bleed out. "This is my body given for you" means simply "This is me for you."

When we come to the Christian Eucharist we come to give our life. We come for self-donation to God and one another. We may be eager or reluctant, but deep in our hearts we know that our desire is to give our life in love. If we could all fit on the altar we would march up together at the Offertory Procession and stand on the altar. Then it would be clear that it is not so much the bread and wine that change; we change. Jesus does not need to change; we need to change. The bread and wine are simply symbols of our life. We cannot live without food or drink. We would not all fit on the altar. God does not want us to open a vein and bleed out. But God does want us to give of our self and to receive God's giving of himself in Jesus, symbolized also by bread and wine, food and drink, the essentials for the maintenance of our life. The Eucharist is about us changing into the Mystical Body of Christ, into Church, into God's life with humankind. Conversion of life is what the Eucharist is about. We become what we eat; we become Christ; we are enabled to act as Christ and to be his hands and feet and heart in this world. We often say "we are what we eat." It means that your healthy life depends on healthy food. We do not take it literally in the sense that if you eat a tomato you become a tomato. But, in the Eucharist we do become what we eat and drink. We are changed. We are converted in our hearts to take on the life of Christ in our human exchange with others. The Eucharist is not so much a gee-whiz event, but a miracle greater than any understanding of "transubstantiation." We are changed, and the human heart is free not to change. The greatest miracle in the world is not creation from nothing "in the beginning," because God is infinitely rich, and creation costs God nothing. The greatest miracle is God's creation of a clean heart from a heart that is mired in negativity, that is free to refuse God's grace, and which is changed without violation of its integrity in the mystery of the Eucharist. It is not a quick change; it is not a guaranteed change. Conversion is, however, the miracle of miracles that is going on in the celebration of the Christian Eucharist and in the other mysterious ways of God's grace worldwide.

We also are told that the blood of Christ is salvific and has washed away our sins. We should not understand such a proposition as a claim that God needed blood, the Shakespearean "pound of flesh," in order to be appeased for the insult of human sinfulness. Better to think of the redemption of sin in this way. Every sin brings a temporal punishment due to sin. Forgiveness of sin is one thing, and God is ever merciful. We still owe for damages done to the community. Our sins affect one another and do harm that needs to be righted in so far as possible. If you are the bull in a china shop, the owner may readily forgive you but then ask you to come in and help clean up and pay up for what you broke. Jesus in his many years of "community service" on earth has cleaned up and paid up for us. His self-donation, valued as it would be in the cosmic scheme of things in the eyes of God, washed away the damage we cannot undo or repay, whatever would be our efforts. Only God can redeem sin fully, and only the conversion of grace can renew the face of the earth, and bring about a new heaven and a new earth. The answer to Job's lament about his innocent sufferings is not primarily to run down the culprits but to look to God's generosity that can make it right with Job in the fullness of eternal life. When all is said and done, there is no justice in this world. We human beings are not going to redeem the sinfulness of human history. However, God's self-donation in the life and death of his son can redeem our destructive lives in all their complexity. "This is my body, given for you." This is me for you. In the Eucharist we enter into that transfiguration with our bodies and we become part of the self-donation that saves the whole world. Conversion, conversion to a life of love, is the greatest miracle of the Eucharist at its heart.

> Now before the festival of the Passover, Jesus knew that his hour had come to depart from this world and go the Father. Having loved his own who were in the world, he loved them to the end . . . . And during supper Jesus, knowing that the Father had given all things into his hands, and that he had come from God and was going to God, got up from the table, took off his outer robe, and tied a towel around himself. Then he poured water

into a basin and began to wash the disciples' feet and to wipe them with the towel that was tied around him. He came to Simon Peter, who said to him, "Lord are you going to wash my feet"? Jesus answered, "You do not know now what I am doing, but later you will understand." Peter said to him, "You will never wash my feet." Jesus answered, "Unless I wash you, you have no share with me." Simon Peter said unto him, "Lord, not my feet only but also my hands and my head"! Jesus said to him, "One who has bathed does not need to wash, except for the feet, but is entirely clean. And you are clean, though not all of you." For he knew who was to betray him; for this reason he said, "not all of you are clean." After he had washed their feet, had put on his robe, and had returned to the table, he said to them, "Do you know what I have done to you? You call me Teacher and Lord -- and you are right, for that is what I am. So if I, your Lord and Teacher, have washed your feet you also ought to wash one another's feet. For I have set you an example, that you also should do as I have done to you. Very truly, I tell you, servants are not greater that their master, nor are messengers greater than the one who sent them. If you know these things, you are blessed if you do them" (Jn 13 1-17).

For I received from the Lord what I also handed on to you, that the Lord Jesus on the night when he was betrayed took a loaf of bread, and when he had given thanks, he broke it and said, "This is my body that is for you. Do this in remembrance of me." In the same way he took the cup also, after supper, saying, "This cup is the new covenant in my blood. Do this, as often as you drink it, in remembrance of me." For as often as you eat this bread and drink the cup, you proclaim the Lord's death until he comes (1 Cor 11: 23-26).

CHAPTER SIXTEEN

God Is Not Finished with Us Yet
– God has Come and Is Still to Come

God is not finished with us yet. God has created us "in the beginning," come to us in the Bethlehem of Judea, and will come again "in the ending" to finish what God has begun and restored in his Son, our Lord Jesus Christ. So Christians believe the end of the world is not one of dire destruction but one of the full coming of the Kingdom of God, which is even now come on earth, for "the kingdom of God is within you" (Lk 17: 21), but then "in the ending" a new heaven and a new earth. Though God is present always and everywhere, and all the more because God has taken this world unto himself in the Son of God made flesh, we are yet troubled all too often by the absence of God. The drama, "Waiting for Godot," a Godot who never comes, struck a cord in the human heart, because it echoes the trial of faith in our time particularly. We are keenly aware of the absence of God, especially in a world that teeters on one catastrophe or another that could emerge in the near future. We yearn for Jesus to come again and finish what God began "in the beginning" from nothing. "In the ending" God will create from everything, from the wheat and the weeds, the good and the bad of this wonderful and terrible world, a new creation, a new heaven and a new earth. Nothing good will be lost. No memory of what we would remember will be gone forever. It will all make sense, and it will all be no longer vulnerable to change and decay. God's life might be a kaleidoscope of one joy greater than the next, but we will not be losing anything to move into this "everything." We long to hear the words of Jesus on the cross: "It is finished," finally fleshed out for the life of the whole world and not just revealed in the earthly sojourn of God in Jesus two thousand years ago.

We cannot be fully happy until everyone, sinner saved and saint preserved by grace, sit together happily and

forever at the banquet table of the Lord, where the bread
that was broken on earth was his life given for us, the ful-
fillment of which is the inner meaning of eternal life. This
is me, the Lord God of all, given for you for all eternity.
How longingly we do await the end of time. The God
who has come and is still coming we must await. Until
everyone is at the table, until everything "in the ending"
has been consumed in the new creation, we yearn for the
coming of the Lord. "Come, Lord Jesus," which phrase
concludes the Christian Scriptures, reveals the cry of the
human heart through the centuries of time.

In the meantime, we are marooned on planet earth,
huddled together in anxiety in lifeboat earth, seemingly
adrift, in a vast, violent, and indifferent cosmos. Our situ-
ation, however, is not without hope. We are poor, but we
have the pledge of God himself in Jesus that God is coming
again. We might be compared to someone who has won
the lottery. The winner is no longer poor. The winner has
the winning ticket in their hand. We have the bread of
eternal life on the tip of our tongue. However, long may
it be before the winner of the lottery has a nickel in their
pockets. Wealth is to come, but it may take months before
anyone sees it. We have God-with-us in the Gospel, in the
Church, in the bread of life, in one another, but it may be

quite a while before we enjoy the treasure we have been given all undeserved and find each other at that same banquet table of the Lord in eternity.

Atop the Golden Dome at the University of Notre Dame, the gold-leaf statue of Mary, the Mother of God, looks down upon the university campus. If you look closely you may notice that the Mary in the statue appears to be pregnant. It might just be my imagination, naivete, or elderly eyesight, but I thought the sculptor of the statue wanted us to know that the birth of Christ was ongoing throughout time. Christ has come, Christ is coming, Christ will come again. We also are born into eternal life from the womb of this earth and this world of time. We must be born again in water and the holy Spirit. God has come "in the beginning" and is still coming, and will come at the last "in the ending."

We know in our bones that God is still coming. We look at this world and all of human history and it appears as a gigantic preparation for an event that never happens. If the grave is the dead-end that claims us all, if the sun is destined to burn out and the earth grow dark and frozen and nothing endures, why all this promise and bloom? A world without God and God's presence has no meaning. A world that God has begun and will finish contains and celebrates "in the ending" every good and true meaning that has ever entered the heart and mind of humankind. We live in such hope. "Eye hath not seen, nor ear heard, neither have entered into the heart of man, the things which God hath prepared for them that love him" (1 Cor 2:9).

> The spirit and the bride say, "Come." And let everyone who hears say, "Come." And let everyone who is thirsty come. Let anyone who wishes take the water of life as a gift. The one who testifies to these things says, "Surely I am coming soon." Amen. Come. Lord Jesus! (Rev 22: 16-17,20)

CHAPTER SEVENTEEN

God Is Never Noisy or Wordy – God Is Silent and of Few Words

Silence befits the infinite God, and the reason is because silence is not empty. Silence is not the absence of sound. Silence is the fullness of sound, the cornucopia of words, the absolute reality that say everything by saying nothing, since any one word, any one sound, subtracts from the fullness of the silence that is a plenum – a fullness that is limited only when a sound is made or a word uttered. God is quiet. You have to really listen actively and composedly if you have any chance of God speaking to you. God is not in noise, nor in a mighty sound, rarely in rushing wind (e.g., for dramatic effect, such as the description of the rushing wind of the Holy Spirit descending upon the apostles at Pentecost in the "Acts of the Apostles" -- a description of the indescribable).

Wind has always been an apt symbol of the presence of God, or more precisely the spirit of God. You cannot see wind; you cannot smell wind even if it may carry a fragrance from something or other. You don't know where wind comes from or when it will blow – pace modern meteorology. In the story of Elijah in the cave where he was hiding from his enemies and waiting upon God, the voice of God is not in the earthquake or the fire. God speaks to him in the gentle breeze, in a soft whisper, in a quiet voice as of a child (1 Kings 19: 11-13). Calm, shy, and quiet was our God when he visited our earth. A baby can make noise, but it is speechless. Jesus came among us unable to speak, and he spent most of his earthly life hidden in Nazareth in a silence, addressing no one on earth in words that would be remembered. Jesus did not shout, whether in Galilee or Jerusalem. His life was his speech. His death created an earthquake, i.e., shook the foundations of our world, but to those around him there was mostly silence. When he spoke his words had power, and as a human being we find God speaking our language.

The Word of God is not wordy. If a poem distills a

great deal of insight and language into a small number of poetical words pregnant with further meanings, that is close to God's speech. In the Word of God, the Son of God in the Christian mystery of the Trinity, all of God's infinite speech is distilled into one Word. After "the word of God" found in the Sacred Scriptures has been proclaimed in our liturgical celebration, we no longer say "This is the word of God," because that wording implies we have just heard an account of God giving us information back, but rather we proclaim simply, "The Word of God," which suggests God speaks now and the words just read are only a small part of how God speaks now in the silence of our minds and hearts.

Those who want a spectacular God will argue for the thunder and the lightening in heaven as ways of under-standing God's speech to humankind. God is awesome and frightening in that representation found sometimes in the Bible and elsewhere. The insight is not the most profound understanding of God, because if the word of God is infinitely powerful, God does not need fireworks or noise, or many words. The centurion would have Jesus heal his servant but he did not want Jesus to inconvenience himself by travel to the sick bed: "Lord, I am not worthy to have you come under my roof; but *only speak the word* (italics mine), and my servant will be healed" (Mt. 8:8).

In the Hebrew Scriptures one may argue that God speaks many words, dictates all kinds of law and commands to Moses, and so forth. So it would seem. The long-suffering Job makes his plea to God for justice, and from the cloud God speaks curt words to Job. In essence Job is told he knows nothing about the awesome ways of the Most High and he should just shut up. And then, strangely, God says nothing more in the Hebrew Scriptures after that encounter with the unanswered plea of suffering Job. The next word God speaks is through Jesus of Nazareth, and the most profound words of Jesus are spoken quietly at his crucifixion and death. "Father, forgive them; for they know not what they do" (Lk 23:34). See also the so-called seven last words of Jesus on the Cross as found in the four gospels, which words might well be summed up in this paraphrase: "I will walk through all of human suffering with you." I would yet argue that the silence of God speaks volumes.

> At that place he [Elijah] came to a cave, and he spent the night there. Then the word of the Lord Came to him, saying, "What are you doing here, Elijah"? He answered, "I have been very zealous for the Lord, the God of hosts; for the Israelites have forsaken your covenant, thrown down your altars and killed your

prophets with the sword. I alone am left, and they are seeking my life, to take it away." He said, "Go out and stand on the mountain before the Lord, for the Lord is about to pass by." Now there was a great wind, so strong that it was splitting mountains and breaking rocks in pieces before the Lord, but the Lord was not in the wind; and after the wind an earthquake; and after the earthquake a fire, but the Lord was not in the fire; and after the fire a sound of sheer silence. When Elijah heard it, he wrapped his face in his mantle and went out and stood at the entrance of the cave. Then there came a voice to him that said, "What are you doing here, Elijah?" (1 Kg. 19: 9-13).

CHAPTER EIGHTEEN

God Is Not Complicated
– God Is Simply One

God is simple, simply one, undivided. Everything about God is God. God has nothing; God is everything. God has "it" all-together. His justice is his love; his love is his justice, and his mercy, and his compassion. Whatever we can say about God, by way of analogy I want to add, it is all and only God we are talking about. The ninety-nine names of God are but one name, which we with our feeble human minds cannot understand without breaking down the divine reality into parts. We divide to conquer. "This is not that" is at the bottom of all our intellectual endeavors. With God it is all one. This is that, the past is the future and it is all now. God is only present. God is only one and simply one. Everything of God is God and only God. God does not have any thing but is every thing. It is that simple. God is at the bottom of everything before anything was a thing and forever after.

What we are saying about God is not simple to understand. We like to say that the whole is more than the sum of its parts. The unity of a living body is one life, even though a complexity of organs interacts in unity to sustain its life. But God is one in a whole different way. There are no differences in God, no organic unity, just pure oneness, all one, alone, yet altogether all-together. God is undivided. God is not busy with one thing following another. Everything is there and everything is now, and there is no such thing as a thing in God. God is simple. Truth is his being and truth is love and love is beauty and beauty is goodness and there is only God, nothing less and nothing more. God is infinite but not complicated, eternal and endless but not numbered. God is all the world that is created, which is yet not God, though it all revolves around and depends on God who might be described as the still center. He dwells in simple silence in which all words are enfolded. His only spoken Word is eternal, and that Word took flesh in time (if Christians are to be believed) and glorified yesterday, today, and forever. There is only one God and that God is one only.

Imagine the dilemma of every poet in our world. They want to concentrate the meaning of what has been experienced. They want to distill the flavor and color of human sensitivity in the most compressed and powerful medley of words that the poet can compose. Would that they could say everything all at once in one beautiful and comprehensive word that includes every facet of the diamond of reality all spoken in one word. Only God is the master poet, however, who has said it all in his one Word, the Word of God, not the words of God, but the Word of God. "God from God, light from light, one substance with the Father." The poet T.S. Eliot captured this sense of all-at-oneness in this oft-quoted phrase, "in the beginning is my end." And the last book of the Bible captures that same sense of from beginning to ending all one. "I am the Alpha and the Omega, says the Lord God, who is and who was and who is to come, the Almighty" (Rev 1:8) and "I am the Alpha and the Omega, the first and the last, the beginning and the end" (Rev 22:13). In God all come full circle.

One may wonder why there is only one God. Pagan religions had many gods in charge of many aspects of human life and patrons of this and that locale. The problem with more than one God is this. If you want to have a God that is infinite, there is no room for another God. If there were two gods, for example, one god would have something the other god does not have. The wars in heaven among the gods described in ancient literature stem from just this weakness. In sum, a God who is sovereign can be only one God, and God alone.

We human beings, though many, also desire desperately to be one. We want to be one with each other and one with the world of trees and oceans, plants and animals. We want our pets to go to heaven. We want to marry more than one lovely person. We want it all. We want to be at one with it all. I want to embrace the beautiful coed walking across the campus on a sunny autumn morning, and the squirrels running up the golden leaves of the maple trees along the path. I want to embrace the wounded in war around the world and the men and women locked in prisons like captives in a zoo. Jesus prayed at the Last Supper our heart's desire as well as his own: "I ask . . . that they may all be one. As you, Father, are in me and I am in you, may they also be in us . . . so that they may be one, as we are one" (Jn 17: 20-22).

Perhaps a fitting conclusion to this quest to describe God as simply one might be to quote a very trenchant passage from John Henry Newman:

> I mean then by the Supreme Being, one who is simply self-dependent, and the only Being who is such; moreover that He is without beginning or Eternal, and the only Eternal; that in consequence He has lived a whole eternity by Himself; and hence that He is all-sufficient, sufficient for His own blessedness and all blessed, and ever blessed. Further, I mean a Being, who having these prerogatives, has the Supreme Good, or rather is the Supreme Good, or has all the attributes of Good in infinite intenseness; all wisdom, all truth, all justice, all love, all holiness, all beautifulness; who is omnipotent, omniscient, omnipresent; ineffably one, absolutely perfect; and such, that what we do not know and cannot even imagine of Him, is far more wonderful than what we do and can. I mean One who is sovereign over His own will and actions, though always according to the eternal Rule of right and wrong, which is Himself. I mean, moreover, that He created all things out of nothing and preserves them every moment . . . . It

[theology] teaches of a Being infinite, yet personal; all blessed, yet ever operative, absolutely separate from the creature, yet in every part of creation at every moment; above all things yet under every thing.

(*The Idea of a University* (London: Longmans & Green, 1896; reprint, University of Notre Dame Press, Notre Dame, Indiana, 1982, pp. 46-47)

CHAPTER NINETEEN

God Is Not Comparable to Anything – God Is Unique Mystery

Dictionaries tell us what words mean, but dictionaries are compiled by noting the usage of words. Dictionaries are descriptive and not prescriptive. Language has a life of its own, and people in their speaking and writing create the meaning of words, which meaning is also open to reversal. The more examples of the use of a word, the more likely an accurate definition will be established, at least for the time being. In the Gospel version of the Lord's Prayer, the word for "daily" (as in "Give us this day our daily bread") is a Greek word, *epiousios*, found no where else in the Scriptures or in any extant Greek literature. Jerome translated the same Greek work as Latin *quotidianum* in the Gospel of Luke, and as Latin *supersubstantialem* in the Gospel of Matthew. The English follows *quotidianum*, even though to give us this day our this-day (daily) bread is redundant. In short, no one knows what *epiousios* means because its usage is unique. So it is with the name of the one and only God. In Hebrew Scriptures God could not be named. God is unique and without name. God belongs to no class, no category. God is sui generis, ineffable and indescribable. God's name and God's nature could not be known by human beings.

We have seen this problem before. If you say you do not believe in God, who and what are you talking about? Do you know enough to know that not any God of any description exists ? From what high viewpoint do you limit the nature of God, who escapes all classification? God is not one more being in the world but bigger. He is not contained by the category of "being," of which he would then be a particular example. God is not one more "being." All beings are in God. God is not in history; history is in God. We propose an answer when we ourselves are the question.

All being and all questions and all answers are already within God, who is not an example of anything but himself -- unique, ineffable, unnamable, infinite, beyond "beyond." To believe in God is not so much a piece of information as an affirmation and confirmation of the mystery of God that we are somehow drawn to trust and not to resist.

In Eden the tempter made this kind of pitch to Eve and Adam: "Hey, listen up, you don't want to be human. Human beings have to work to eat and study to learn. They get tired, they get sick, they have their hearts broken in love. And then they up and die. You do not want to be human. You want to be like the Gods, who never die and who enjoy honey and nectar served in a gold cup." Big mistake! By trying to become like God human beings were no more divine in their activity and much less human. Sin is just that kind of nonsense, as we have noted above. God is ineffable and unapproachable mystery, and what God is in himself and of himself we will never know until then, "For now we see through a glass, darkly; but then face to face: now I know in part: but then shall I know even as also I am known" (1 Cor 13:12). What we can know now is what God is for us, not what God is in the mystery of his Godliness.

Christians speak of God as Father, Son, and Holy Spirit. Not three, but one and only one God, whose inner and personal life we can only glimpse and would know nothing about were it not for the mystery of Christianity itself, which holds Jesus as fully both human and divine. Yet, Jesus is not the Father who "so loved the world, that he gave his only begotten Son, that whosoever believes in him should not perish, but have everlasting life. For God sent his Son into the world not to condemn the world, but that the world through him might be saved" (Jn. 3: 16).

How would this Christian mystery of God look if one were to tell only of what God in three divine Persons might be for us -- God for us, not God in God's self. In Jesus we know something of God for us, for Jesus came to us precisely for us and for our salvation, which salvation encompasses the salvation of the world. We might readily understand God the Father as God the Father Almighty, creator of heaven and earth, giver of all good gifts in all their abundance and beauty. In creation of the world, however, God gave of us infinite riches that are inexhaustible, but we do not know or see how God gave himself for us. We know the difference between a benefactor who has given generously of his or her goods, and a spouse, who has given his self or her self to us totally. Jesus is God's self-gift to us. In giving us his son, God has given us every-thing, however unpacked, and even here and now. The Holy Spirit reveals the on-going presence of Jesus Christ in our world after his death and resurrection. The Spirit given Christians in baptism, and to all people of good will in the inner sanctum of their souls when they seek God, provides God's presence here and now, lest we miss the treasure that remains God's coming into our world as one of us in order to enable us as to be somehow one with him. The Holy Spirit is the personal and tender mercy of God that provides for us all, believers and unbelievers alike, the reception of God's grace. The Holy Spirit dwells in the child of God as in a temple, and the Holy Spirit acts within us spiritually by illumining our minds and enkindling our hearts. The Holy Trinity is revealed to us as God-for-us, just as the bread of the Eucharist reveals "This is my body given for you." In short, "This is me for you."

> In the beginning was the Word, and the Word was with God, and the Word was God. He was in the be-ginning with God. All things came into being through him, and without him not one thing came into being. What has come into being in him was life, and the life was the light of all people. The light shines in the dark-ness, and the darkness did not overcome it.

There was a man sent from God, whose name was John. He came as a witness to testify to the light, so that all might believe through him. He himself was not the light, but he came to testify to the light. The true light, which enlightens everyone, was coming into the world.

He was in the world, and the world came into being through him; yet the world did not know him. He came to what was his own, and his own people did not accept him. But to all who received him, who believed in his name, he gave power to become children of God, who were born, not of blood or of the will of the flesh, or of the will of man, but of God.

And the Word became flesh and lived among us, and we have seen his glory, the glory of a father's only son, full of grace and truth. John testified to him and cried out, "This was he of whom I said, He who comes after me ranks ahead of me because he was before me." From his fullness we have all received, grace upon grace. The law indeed was given through Moses; grace and truth came through Jesus Christ. No one has ever seen God. It is God the only Son, who is close to the Father's heart, who has made him known. (Jn 1: 1-18)

CHAPTER TWENTY

God Is Not Comprehendible – God Is Ineffable

Who would want a God cut down to our size? What kind of an infinite God could it be that we could wrap around our limited and often mistaken rational mind. As Woody Allen once quipped: "I wouldn't belong to a club that would have me as a member." God is not made in our image; we are made in God's image, and a very humble and finite image we are. Being in God's image is no small thing, however, and we do know something by way of analogy about the mystery of God.

God is good and we are too. God acts with goodness and sometimes we do as well act with goodness. Our goodness is not identical to God's goodness. In fact our goodness, or truth, or beauty, or whatever quality we share in some way with God, only approximates the awesomeness of God in whom all qualities are simply God. God is existence, is goodness, is truth, and so forth. We have a version of existence, of goodness, of truth, and so forth. We are made in God's image and there is a likeness, but a likeness that a creature of God can only approach as holy ground. Yet, we are not altogether different from God without any common ground that our minds and hearts can comprehend Our trouble begins when we turn things upside down and decide to make God in our own image. Our depictions of God depict our own predicament and behaviors all too often. Because we are judgmental and vindictive, for example, we lay that character on to God, who must be vindictive and punitive like us but much bigger and more fearsome. God might well conclude: "With friends like that, who needs enemies." The entire book before the reader was undertaken precisely to undo the mistaken depictions of God based on God in our own image, and to try to allow God to emerge as a loving mystery, acting toward us with only love beyond imagining -- a God worthy of being loved and adored.

When Moses speaks with God revealed to him at the sight of the "burning bush" in the *Book of Exodus*, he asks God a question: "If I come to the Israelites and say to them, 'The God of your ancestors has sent me to you,' and if they ask me 'What is his name? What shall I say to them'? God said to Moses, 'I am who I am.' " (Ex: 3: 13-14)

> In the year King Uzziah died, I saw the Lord sitting on a throne, high and lofty; and the hem of his robe filled the temple. Seraphs were in attendance above him; each had six wings: with two they covered their faces, and with two they covered their feet, and with two they flew. And one called to another and said: "Holy, holy, holy is the Lord of hosts; the whole earth is full of his glory." The pivots on the threshold shook at the voices of those who called, and the house was filled with smoke. (Is 6: 1-4)

> I would like to beg you dear Sir, as well as I can, to have patience with everything unresolved in your heart and to try to love the questions themselves as if they were lock rooms or books written in a very foreign language. Don't search for the answers, which could not be given

to you now, because you would not be able to live them. And the point is to live everything. Live the questions now. Perhaps then, someday far in the future, you will gradually, without even noticing it, live your way into the answer.

Rainer Maria Rilke in *Letters to a Young Poet.*

CHAPTER TWENTY-ONE

God Is Not the Problem
– God Is the Solution

In this book the argument remains that the inadequate depictions of God are responsible in large part for the denial of God. Bad arguments for the existence of God and the bad example of believers in God have done more to spur unbelief in God than any other kind of reason. The problem we have seen before. If you say you do not believe in God, we need to know what that word God means and connotes for you, for if that understanding of God is mistaken, any positive outcome is undermined.

Nevertheless, even the best description of God that any believer would wish to suggest may not persuade. Understandably the objection could be made that we are begging the question of the existence of God, that is, assuming God's existence to be true. That is what must first be proven. To argumentation for the existence of God I want to give both a short response and a long response. Short response: By far most of the people of the world, in so far as we have a history of human behavior, have believed in God, and in that number are included numerous persons of the highest intelligence, education, and notable moral virtue. Argument from numbers is not the best of arguments, however, even though I want to claim that the burden of unbelief falls to those who deny the existence of God. They are swimming upstream, but that in inself does not make them wrong. The long response I break down into four considerations for affirming the existence of God, for better or for worse, and worse leads to deserved unbelief and better leads to thoughtful belief, but still belief. There never will be a scientific proof for the existence of God, for God as spiritual cannot be observed in the ways germane to all empirical science.

Before examining the four arguments that I think are

worthy of consideration of the question of God, let me say something about human knowing. There are conclusions that I know that I know. There are conclusions that I know I do not know. We also know more than we know that we know, or at least, more than we can tell. What is dangerous for all of us remains that we do not know what we do not know. However, we are quick to claim we have an objective viewpoint, the "view from nowhere." We might have a view from where we are, this time and place, our body and soul, our education and experience. The view from everywhere would be more like God's viewpoint than our human mind, which mind has little reason to believe it stands in judgment of God or is proportioned to the task of understanding God and God's ways. And finally, if you want to remain skeptical and claim human beings cannot know anything for sure, you cannot claim that the one thing we can know is that we cannot know.

Here are the four considerations I would put before the reader for why I think the existence of God could be presumed as a basic affirmation from which an adequate or inadequate depiction of God would carry some weigh of argument for or against belief in God. (1) If you begin with "I am here, where is God," you are off to a slow start.

If you begin with assuming your existence is self-explained and self-justified, and it is God who needs to be explained, you are courting trouble. If you begin with I am the solution and God is the problem, you may still find a way to God, but it is the long way round. Better to begin with a deep humility and with the belief of the soldier in the foxhole. I cannot guarantee my survival. I cannot explain my existence, I do not know who I am or what I am, I remain always and everywhere fragile and vulnerable. I am next to nothing, I need not exist, and there is no godless explanation of why anything, and all the more, why me. I am not the existential solution, for which God's existence is the problem. I am the problem for which God is the solution. To me that is how I would begin if I want to maximize my chances of finding some truth about God.

Let me repeat my argument. How not to believe in God? Start off on the wrong foot. Claim God is the problem and you are the solution. Claim the high ground. I am here; where is God? Must be there is no God. In truth we are the problem for which God is the solution. We are the mystery on which God sheds light. God is the one who is here and everywhere, more part of me than I myself. The question is who am I, why me, why anything, and where am I going. Start there. I did not make myself, or this world, nor do I have any necessity to exist. My life is contingent and vulnerable, my mind limited and undeveloped, my activity all too often blind and self-seeking. Who and what is God? No, begin with who and what am I?

(2) The argument from causality is surely prominent in philosophical argument for the existence of God. In one form or another the claim is that from nothing comes nothing. There has to be a beginning, a necessary existence from which all other existence takes its origin. Why anything? Why "why" of the two-year maddening child is a question seemingly hard-wired in our human mind. If the ancient myth has it that the world is held up on the back of a giant turtle, one can ask what holds that turtle up, and to claim it is "turtles all the way down" is a good bit of verbal humor, but it only underlines the question. What accounts for the existence of anything and everything? Material explanations tell us a good deal about the "how" of it all, but little about the "why." Consciousness itself presents a phenomenon not reducible to bits of matter in infinite arrangement and interaction. I know that I know that I know, and there is no end to the sequence. As with moral conscience, many thoughtful people argue that matter will

not explain what looks more and more like spirit. If God is anything, God is spirit. And so the quest for God with an appeal to some argument from causality is a promising quest, though it has never convinced all the people of philosophical intelligence and good will. It surely ought to give pause to everyone. Once again I want to claim that I respect the agnostic more than the atheist who claims he knows there is no God. Really. How ever would you know that? To turn the table, there is no universally convincing argument for the non-existence of God.

(3) If you consider this rare earth, planet of a thousand adjustments that had to go just right for our life to be what it is, odds are better that you would win the lottery tomorrow. It is harder to believe the materialistic story of planet earth than it is to believe in a God who somehow intended it all from the beginning, however it was all to unfold in the violent upheavals of the cosmos. My argument is not the "argument from design," though it has similarities. I want to say stay struck with wonder. There has to be a whole lot more than what meets the eye and no end in sight. My argument is the argument from confluence of suspicions that planet earth is part of something very big and at bottom more than mere chance. Again I want to say

it is easier to believe in God that in the roll of astronomical dice, given this world's awesome kaleidoscope.

(4) Belief in God is best understood as not a piece of information. Question: is there a God? Answer: yes or no. Belief in God turns out to be trust in God, and the heart has reasons the mind knows not of, as Pascal said so well long ago. If I have already decided there cannot be a God, my probing is compromised. Where your heart is there is your treasure. Do I have an interest in a no-God outcome? Maybe I do, even unconsciously. The prayer, "Lord, I believe, help my unbelief," tells of a deep down willingness. Can the question of God be divorced from the implications of belief in God. It all will impact the way I live. In Dostoyevsky's great novel, *Brothers Karamazov*, the wise monk Zosima is approached by a rich lady who says she has lost all faith in God. The wise man does not give her an argument but a task. "Go and serve the poor, and your faith will revive."

I do not want to say anyone who does not believe in God has a moral defect or is willful about unbelief. I do want to say the whole person is involved, and that only God knows what we believe. I do think that our words about God might be misleading to others and to ourselves.

I am inclined to follow someone around for a day and watch how he or she walks the walk and not just how they talk the talk. Belief in God may well be in our bones, in our activities, kind or unkind, in our heart, and not just in our logic and its rational conclusions. I am overwhelmed with what I understand and what I do not understand, with what I have and what I do not have, with what this life gives and what it does not give. Stay tuned is what I want to say. God (if there is a God) is surely not finished with us yet. Stay tuned. If there is not a God, however would you know for sure? Belief in God may just in the end depend more on God than on us.

Epilogue

The thesis of this book has been simple. Arguments against God are often based on a mistaken depiction of God that disaffects those who come to believe in God but lukewarmly, as well as those who cannot believe at all in such a God as has been presented to them by the ignorance of others or their own. Arguments against God, either in his very existence or in his approachability, are often based on depiction of a false God that does not exist. Arguments for God, alas, often fall short of persuasion, for whatever our understanding of God, it is based not on seeing God face to face in this world but on analogy with what we do see in this world. We are made in the image of God, and something but not everything of God can be found in human beings and indeed in the created world around us. All too often we return the favor and make God in our own image, and that is where the misunderstanding and distortion takes its origin.

Moreover, we cannot communicate our understanding of anything profound without ambiguity, because our own speech is imperfect and our listeners' interpretative ability limited as well. Maybe we should conclude our considerations of the pro and con of "who God is" with a paradox I once coined to begin each class with my students: "I do not always say what I mean; I do not always mean what I say, and what you heard is not what I said." We believers and unbelievers alike can say these words, for we know not what we do or say in any profound way. "Father, forgive them, for they do not know what they are doing" echoes in my mind (Lk 23: 34). We are not in a position to pass judgment on God. We need to embrace our own mystery in the hope that it will help us acknowledge God's mystery. We are not in a position to pass judgment on one another, nor even, and maybe especially, upon our selves. In truth, I do not always say what I mean, nor mean what I say, and what you heard may well not be what I said. Out of what pain, out of what "cloud of unknowing" do we speak? I am hardly judge of myself, much less the judge of the mystery of another person caught up in the mystery of God.

Perhaps it would be helpful to point out the same predicament in the life of Jesus himself. You can see his struggle with belief, and perhaps more accurately I should say his struggle with trust in God. I think one could assume Jesus believed in God, as almost everyone in ancient times did, but that if he had any questions similar to our modern questioning of God's existence or of God's approachability, the question of Jesus would have been: "Am I God's beloved"? Does God care for me and in any special way"? It is really the same question for our contemporary seeker. Does God exist and does God care for me are basically the same question, because if you parse the word God exhaustively it includes a love for all his creation and in particular for each and every human being made in his image. The emphasis is different, of course, but the underlying question remains. Is there a God, and we presume a good and loving God in order there be a God worthy of the word?

There seems to be four crisis points in the public ministry of Jesus leading up to his death. (1) I would argue that Jesus heard a voice or had some inner experience at his baptism that the Gospel evangelist translates in these words spoken by God: "This is my Son, the Beloved, with whom I am well pleased" (Mt 3: 17). In the strength of that revelation Jesus began his public ministry of preaching and healing. The Kingdom of God has come, and Jesus was the prophet of the new kingdom, a kingdom within us even now and then to come in its fullness "in the ending." (2) That assurance of divine care and love was tested on Mt. Tabor when Jesus spent the night in prayer before deciding to go up to Jerusalem, even though his enemies were awaiting him. (3) That assurance of divine care and love was tested again and under similar circumstances as Jesus prayed through the night in the Garden of Gethsemani. Again his close friends among his apostles fell asleep. Again Jesus is assured God is with him. (4) The final test of the presence of God takes place as Jesus is dying on Calvary hill: "He saved others; he cannot save himself. He is the King of Israel; let him come down from the cross now, and we will believe in him. He trusts in God; let God deliver him now, if he wants to; for he said, 'I am God's Son' " (Mt 27: 42-43). In short, if you [Jesus]are, as you claim, the beloved of God, what are you doing in such a predicament? Maybe you are not beloved of God. Looks that way!

We think our age is unique in its experience of the absence of God, and surely the felt absence of God is intense in our time. Whatever the spiritual climate, however, every man and woman must pass through the darkness, through the loneliness, and through the death of the body. In all those moments the question is "where is God"? No amount of written argument can spare one the lived experience of faith and hope in God whose love we must trust wholeheartedly to the end.

One might ask if the quest for God and the hope to depict God in a way that is most helpful would be the same quest for all the world religions. Christians are hardly the only seekers or believers. There are four possible responses to the problem of the multiple understandings of who God is and what are his ways. (1) You can assume your religion is the only true religion and everyone else remains in error, some more and some less. It is a position taken at some time through the centuries by most religions. We are right, everyone else is wrong. But the position is arrogant and presumptive that others are not also intelligent and spiritual. God's grace is given to all human beings in some way. (2) You can assume that no one is right and that the truth about God escapes us all. Or, you can assume everyone is right and no one can judge. But that position is skeptical and basically gives up on the truth being attainable, and on some beliefs more worthy of God than others. (3) You can assume that were all religions to purify their beliefs and the ways that they teach and express them to others, we would be able to take everything that is good, true, and beautiful from each and every religion. The truth is not in competition with itself. There is only one truth, and it is a very wide umbrella properly proposed. But such a position is unsustainable, because just when human beings work through all the purification of their belief and its expression in words, they age and die, and we begin over again with the young who cannot be given the wisdom of the ages so easily. (4) You can assume that God might want things to remain in flux with no resolution of our differences in world religions. God might want us to love one another, even if we do not come to see each other as the same, and even if we cannot agree with each other. The final resolution of our differences may just have to wait for the fullness of the coming of the Kingdom of God, and in the meantime we may be asked to speak politely and humbly to each other, and despite our differences in thought and rhetoric to love each other well and to work together to assuage human suffering. In the end all of our plans depend on divine providence and God is not impotent in these matters. St. Paul recognized that "in the ending" Jews and Christians would be of one belief, but he did not know when or how. What he trusted was God's love and care, for the "chosen people," who were still the chosen people in the heart of God's love, a love that does not change. Other religions share in that same divine largesse.

Whenever we say we believe in God or we do not believe in God, we love God or we do not love God, one still wants always and everywhere to ask what exactly do we mean by the word "God." Misleading or mistaken descriptions of God that disaffect us may be hidden in our somewhat careless and sometimes reckless descriptions of God, who deserves better. Please God!